# HOW TO MAKE A REVOLUTION

# HOW TO MAKE
# A REVOLUTION

## RAYMOND POSTGATE

WESTHOLME
Yardley

Westholme Publishing, LLC
904 Edgewood Road
Yardley, Pennsylvania 19067
Visit our Web site at www.westholmepublishing.com

ISBN: 978-1-59416-303-6
Also available as an eBook.

Printed in the United States of America.

# CONTENTS

# PART I—THE PROBLEM STATED

## CHAPTER I

### SCIENTIFIC METHODS OF INVESTIGATION

THE object of this book is not to persuade people that a drastic social change is needed. A very large number of books with that object have been written already; and the course of events is acting as a far more powerful propagandist. Nor is it to investigate the causes of the misery of society, their development and the " long term " methods by which they can be cured. This knowledge is immediately necessary to-day, but it is found in such books as G. D. H. Cole's *Guide Through World Chaos*, to which the reader is referred.

The object of this book is to answer, as scientifically as possible, the question: " How can a change be brought about ? " Given that the readers of this book desire a thorough social change, and that they have some adequate idea of the measures that radical reformers should apply when once in power, there still remains the question: " How can power be taken over ? How can a revolution, peaceful or otherwise—for it would be unscientific to limit our investigations by sentimental barriers—be carried through ? "

7

It is quite possible that the answer is: " It cannot be, by any means." More people than is generally realized are, by the force of continual disillusionments, accepting that answer in fact. If we may summarize their argument, spoken or unspoken, it would run as follows: " No constitutional party has ever made a drastic change. No nominally revolutionary party has ever approached power through ordinary political means without losing all its power and drive. Whatever be the reason of that, it is a universal disease. And as for non-constitutional means —well, any fool can see that no rising of the oppressed stands a chance to-day.

" Since there's no help, let's not talk about it. It may be we are all rushing to destruction—to war, or some form of gangster-Nazi rule, or utter collapse and universal slums and unemployment. But since we can do nothing, let us enjoy what we can while we can."

Perhaps this is true; but at least such a conclusion should not be accepted till methods have been seriously and scientifically investigated. It is some time since any such investigation was made. This book is intended to be such.

An investigation should be conducted by experts. The writer of this, in offering his credentials as an expert, will merely say that for fifteen years his chief study has been the patient investigation of revolutionary movements since 1763. An inquiry of this kind should presumably be based on an analysis of the history of past revolutionary movements; and also upon the analysis of the theories of revolutionary change that have arisen in the course of revolutions. The writer believes himself qualified to write, shall we say, the prolegomena at least to such a study.

It is further necessary for anyone who proposes to make this study, and expects to be taken seriously, to say what measure of exactitude he hopes to achieve in his results. At the risk of being pedantic, then, the conditions of our investigation must be stated.

First of all, the degree of exactitude that can be hoped for is not high. Sciences like arithmetic can claim an absolute certainty for their results. Two and two are always four. Not so with us. There are many unavoidable elements of error.

The first element of error that will be found to enter into our calculation is due to the variability and shifty nature of the material. We are dealing with the actions of human beings in certain circumstances. We are not likely to know all the circumstances, and even if we did human behaviour is to a certain extent impredictable. All exact knowledge is dependent upon one thing—the repeatability of experiments. If it is doubted that Boyle's Law is valid, then Boyle's experiment can be repeated, and repeated again and again till every student's doubt is dispersed. But in a study of revolutionary tactics no experiment can ever be repeated. We know as a fact that, however great may be the similarity of certain details, no revolutionary experience will ever really be reproduced in identical conditions and between identical forces. Certain minor events may indeed recur so frequently that a fairly sure technique can be, and has been, deduced from them. Local restricted strikes have occurred so often that experienced trade union officials (and employers) know how to handle them and have evolved certain rules of thumb—as for example, that it is most unwise to call a strike with less than a two-thirds majority in favour. When this rule is ignored, as in France in 1920, disaster follows speedily.

But such instances are few, and confined to limited problems. Great changes, such as those we are considering, occur but once or twice in a century and always in greatly varying circumstances.

The second element is one that is more dangerous. For the impulse to error, here, lies within ourselves. Dear Brutuses, we are servants of our wishes and our indolence. We are studying a subject in which we are not disinterested. We almost all wish consciously or unconsciously that our sums shall end in an answer that is already chosen in our minds. Other sciences are not free from wish-thinking. The study, for example, of the effects of alcohol on the human body is an investigation which surely should, in theory at least, be susceptible of rigorous scientific investigation. But a very brief perusal of prohibitionist or anti-prohibitionist literature shows that it is not so in fact. Dr. Raymond Pearl, the famous biologist of Johns Hopkins University, some time ago conducted an inquiry which appeared to show that, in certain parts of Baltimore City, moderate drinking gave a slightly higher probability of longevity than complete tee-totalism. But the vituperative reception of this conclusion showed that either Dr. Pearl or his critics, or both, were wish-thinking and suffering from a vision distorted by their personal preferences for drinking wine or soft drinks. Even in physics, surely an exact science, it has been charged against Sir James Jeans and Sir Arthur Eddington that their best-known books are vitiated by a desire, evident to all but themselves, that their conclusions should be such that the existence of God could be proved from them.

Far more, then, are *we* likely to fall into error. Most of us desire to prove that a satisfactory change may be brought about without bloodshed and violence. For those of us who have any serious interest in the matter of all, this is a very passionate wish indeed. We must, therefore, if we hope to be impartial investigators at all, weight our conclusions against ourselves. We must adopt what, for convenience's sake, can be best described as a " pessimistic attitude." We must—since we cannot evaluate these probabilities in exact terms—incline to disbelieve whatever we would naturally wish to believe, and whenever we think we have reached a favourable conclusion, put against it an apparently arbitrary mark of scepticism.

If this be accepted, there follows yet another conclusion, which I can best express by saying that there must always be a double expression of the results that we reach—an esoteric and a public statement. We may reach a certain " pessimistic " conclusion as to the probabilities of the success of a certain method of revolution. We may, in the seclusion of our study, decide that success is improbable, but possible; and that the ratio of probability is not so heavily against it as to debar our attempting to use it. But to announce this conclusion in these terms in public propaganda at once disarranges one at least of the factors on which we have been calculating. For one of these factors must be the confidence of the outside world in the probable success of our chosen method. No politician, Fascist or Communist or any other, can with any hope of success announce to his followers and to the general public: " Follow me in this path of revolution. The chances are two to one against us, but maybe it's worth gambling on them." His army will dissolve.

Effectively, such a principle has always been followed by serious revolutionary leaders. Even those who have most prided themselves on exact and dispassionate statement—Lenin and his immediate entourage—have done the same. It is true that Lenin is credited with an aphorism at the time of the Polish war: " Always take a one-in-three chance of revolution." But this remark—if it was made—was made in a discussion at a subcommittee of the Communist International. It was not made as part of an address to Tugachevsky's battalions during their advance on Warsaw.

Even after these elements of error have been allowed for, there remain certain factors which will have to be regarded as unknowable. They will have to be entered, as it were, as *x*. They must be treated, empirically, as static, for since we cannot know if and when they will rise or fall we have no other way of treating them. This does not mean that they are unimportant. Far from it: they may indeed turn out to be crucial.

These factors, which we are calling either unknown or unknowable, deal chiefly with the probable response of individuals to economic or political stimuli. For example, it is frequently alleged that the Negro or American-Indian races fail to respond as intelligently or courageously to oppression as white races. But if such racial differences exist, they certainly have not been studied.

It is argued again that progressive deterioration (or amelioration) of stocks by uncontrolled selection is destroying (or increasing) legitimate hopes of social progress. But it is sure that genetical studies have not yet advanced sufficiently to provide an answer.

Nor are the effects of floods, famines, or wars at all sufficiently known for us to generalize from them. It is often stated, for example, that the generation which is now between thirty and forty-five was so decimated by the Great War that it is unable to reconstruct the world as it should. But it has never been investigated, and perhaps cannot be, whether the war in fact killed off more Sorleys and Rupert Brookes than it did thugs and degenerates.

Finally, among the uncertain factors must be counted the reactions of masses of human beings to the wireless and other forms of propaganda. It is clear that this can be very great. It can not only induce large bodies of men to believe that other large bodies are their natural enemies and almost devoid of human qualities, it can temporarily at least stop the working of some of the most elementary human instincts. It can, with the police absent, actually persuade a hungry man that it is wrong to steal bread for himself or his family. That its effects are unknowable cannot be argued; but it is true that they have not at present been studied practically by any but a few advertising experts, and that the conclusions and practice of these experts are not on the whole relevant to our purposes.

These qualifications do not mean that no knowledge at all is possible. They merely mean that our conclusions can only be approximate and of varying validity. We may perhaps be able to say at the end that action $x$ is more likely to lead to a successful revolution than action $y$; we are fairly likely to be able to say that action $z$ is almost certain not to do so.

The method of study, or at least of exposition, should no doubt ideally be the method which is in fact followed by the first investigators. Starting with no more than a general inclination towards social change we should amass all data which appeared likely to be relevant to our end. We should recount in luxuriant detail the stories of all recorded revolutions—luxuriant because at this point of time we should not know what details were significant and what were not. We should then examine this imposing mass of phenomena and see if from them arose any coherent plan or ordered system. We should be able fairly swiftly, then, to apply our encyclopedic information as a check to the systems of revolutionary theory that we should then begin to study, and should in a short time, though not without a rather tedious citing of instances, be able to decide which of them, if any, remained valid to-day.

But such a method, superior and indeed essential in actual investigation, is impracticable when we come to exposition. The details of revolutionary history are peculiar, immensely interesting and often astonishing, but they are too vast to be included in a small study. Thirty volumes are necessary for the library of the student who wishes to investigate the Paris Commune alone; the mere enumeration of the fantastic and possibly significant incidents of the Russian or French revolutions would require a number which is probably almost astronomical. For the purposes of elucidation we are forced to turn the logical method upside down. We must first investigate revolutionary theories, and then enumerate and study the occasions on which they have been applied, or brought near to application.

Even here we must allow of some deviation from the ideal. Theoretically, the perfect instrument of revolution may be hidden away in the obscure writings of a sociologist whom accident deprived of his just influence. It is not probable; but the deeply conscientious student—had he but world enough and time—would not be satisfied till all economists and political philosophers had been thoroughly searched.

In the early 'sixties, for example, the First International had its attention momentarily called to the theories of a philosopher named Jacques Guillaume Claude Alexandre Hippolyte Colins. He advocated, it appears, a combination of small holdings and compulsory atheism. It is quite possible that, secreted in the nineteen volumes of this polyonymous and Victorian Belgian, is hidden the key to the solution of our troubles. It is possible, but hardly probable. We are forced, since we are dealing with an immediate problem, to make a choice of rough common sense, and study only those theories which have had a sufficient influence on the actions of men either to be applied or to make some considerable body of persons attempt to apply them.

It will probably be found, therefore, that revolutionary theories, thus limited, fall into no more than three general categories. The first is Marxism, and its development, Leninism; the second is industrial unionism, or syndicalism; the third is a theory of direct action by picked bodies of men, which in history has two main forms, called generally anarchism and Blanquism. The last is an almost forgotten theory, yet has, for all that, some surprising successes to recommend it.

# Part II—THEORY

## CHAPTER II

### MARXISM, FASCISM, LENINISM

Of theories of revolution, there is no doubt which is the premier to-day. Marxism is not only the theory which has had more followers than any other theory for many years now; it is also the only non-Fascist theory which has led to a revolution in fact. The Russian Revolution was not only directed by Marxists in accordance with what they considered to be Marx's instructions, but after its success its leaders have retained a peculiar veneration for its philosopher, and all social studies—indeed all human life as far as may be—are conducted in Russia in accordance with his principles.

The vast mass of Marx's writings, and the far vaster mass of commentary—a body of writing most of which is very difficult reading and some of which is very unprofitable when read—make it impossible here to give a full analysis of his theories. Fortunately, however, it is not absolutely necessary to do so. Our inquiry has a particular object—to discover what are and what are not practical instruments of revolution to-day. We need only investigate those aspects of Marxism which have a bearing on that

17

B

question. We can pass by all other aspects, however important they may be either as criticisms of society to-day or as guides for the society of to-morrow.

The Marxist system, roughly, may be said to divide itself most easily into three main portions—the dialectic; pure economic theory; and the theory of historical materialism.

The first-named, the dialectic, is in the opinion of orthodox Marxists the most important part of Marxism, and the groundwork of everything else. It is claimed to be a necessary instrument of thought. Whether that be so or not, the practical revolutionary —practical in the limited sense in which that word is used here—passes it by. The dialectic is a method of philosophical statement, a development of Hegelianism which in theory is essential for a grasp of the process of revolutionary change, but in fact is not so, even though Marx himself declared it indispensable.

It is difficult, without being unjust, to explain it in simple language. Perhaps it can best be understood if we first consider the pre-Hegelian method of arguing. That is based upon definition and exclusion. The State is the State; the Earth is the Earth; and so forth. Further, the State is, let us say, Monarchical. If it is not Monarchical, it is not a State. The Earth is round; if it is not round, it is not the Earth. There are no half-way houses; no confusions. Against this the dialectic method proclaims that truth is never discovered by such means. It is arrived at by the clash of two opposites. Out of that clash comes the truth. Everything is changing, there are no fixities. The State is Monarchical. But proceed: the State is also Democratic. The two clash—or at least appear to, though the democratic state arises out of its enemy, the monarchical state. From their clash will arise another state, the proletarian.

This pattern of (1) a proposition, (2) a contradiction and (3) a reconciliation of the two is called: Thesis—Antithesis—Synthesis. Putting it in general terms we may say: There are certain social and natural objective conditions (*thesis*). From these arise human needs and human purposes, which in recognizing the possibilities in the said objective conditions (*antithesis*), give rise to the *synthesis*, which is a course of action calculated to realize these possibilities. The dialectic, as a further proof of its own truth, calls on us to observe that all changes from one social system or set of conditions to another, show three linked characteristics. The first is *unity* between the two phases. Certain features are always preserved, the Marxist alleges; as for example communism will preserve technical forms of industrial development taken from capitalism. The second is *difference* between the two phases. Certain characteristics of the first phase are destroyed—such as the legal relation known as private property. The third is *complete novelty*: there appear new forms of organization of human life which, although they arise from the past, so change the significance of the survivals as to give them a new meaning and character. A wholly new system appears which cannot be analysed down into mere combination of old elements.

From this point the cycle starts again. Social institutions again (*thesis*) exist: again they produce needs (*antithesis*): again these needs produce their natural result in new relations and organization in society (*synthesis*). And so on, presumably, for ever and ever and ever. The strict Marxist will add that this system applies also to biology and the physical sciences. It has even been asserted that the boiling of water can only be explained by the dialectic. This peculiar pattern-of-three, a sort of trinitarian formula, is imprinted on much modern scientific work in Russia. An example is A. Nemilov's *The Biological Tragedy of Woman*, an account of woman's physical disabilities which attempts spasmodically to follow it, and apologizes in its preface for apparent deviations. It does not appear that Mr. Nemilov's thought has been clarified or assisted by it. Indeed it seems as though he was arbitrarily endeavouring to class all the phenomena of female life, from lactation to menstruation, into a three-cornered pattern merely for the sake of artistic symmetry. . . .

Nor is it likely that we shall find ourselves clarified or assisted in thought by it. In selecting methods of revolutionary activity we may, if successful, find that we have chosen a method which fits into a pattern of thesis, antithesis and synthesis; and that fact may give us philosophical satisfaction. But we shall not make that discovery till afterwards: indeed, it may only be made for us, when we are dead, by a professor in Utopia. As a criterion for picking out a method of change the dialectic is as useless to us as it would have been to a *sansculotte* sharpening pikes. It is almost impossible for us to know whether or not a given method is in a world pattern an antithesis: it is quite impossible to prove that another method is *not* an antithesis. If we reply: " Oh, no: what we must do is to prove that such and such a method is the *correct* antithesis," then we are forced to inquire what is the meaning of " correct." We have then to abandon the dialectic and settle the problem of " correctness " by technical considerations of the difficulties of the immediate problem; just as the pike-sharpener, not knowing the dialectic, inspected his grindstone.

With slightly more hesitation, we may reject also the whole system of Marxian economics—pure economics, that is to say. It is not necessary to assume that strict Marxian economics are untrue. It is only necessary to say that any other system of economics, which has any relation to the circumstances of to-day, admits for us the necessary facts. A recent brief summary of Marx's economics says :

" Labour-power is bought and sold; the capitalist must buy it because it is an essential factor of production, and the labourer must sell it because he has no other means of living. But the conditions of the bargain are essentially unequal; for the capitalist, by virtue of the accumulated capital at his command, is able to appropriate to himself the main benefits of the increase in productivity which comes from large-scale production and the division of labour. The labourer gets paid for the individual effort which he

puts in at a rate determined by the higgling of the
market; but when labour becomes more productive
as a result of an improvement in its technical utiliza-
tion, the main advantage of this increased productivity goes to the capitalist in the form of profits
rather than to the worker. The workers may indeed
by combination do something to get for themselves a
share in the benefits of increasing productivity; and,
where labour is scarce in relation to the demand for
it, real wages may rise even in the absence of effective
combination. But there is an inherent tendency,
according to the Marxians, in the capitalist system to
allot a disproportionate share of the growing productivity of the economic system to rent, interest and
profits, and to exploit the labourer by paying him too
little in relation to the productivity of his efforts."
(G. D. H. Cole : *Intelligent Man's Guide Through
Chaos*, p. 594.)

The bare bones of this are largely recognized as a real
skeleton by most economists: the flesh laid upon them
is often rejected. It is frequently, for example,
claimed that Marx's analysis of " constant " and
" variable " capital is incorrect. A " great contradiction " was long ago discovered in the more elaborate
superstructure of his theory, and his whole concept
of surplus value has been gravely challenged.

But it is precisely this superstructure which is
to-day utterly unimportant. Two essential state-
ments of fact rise out of Marxian economics and they
happen to be two that are provable by any system of
economics which is not obviously feeble-minded wish-
thinking. The first is that capital is fairly rapidly

*concentrating.* It is universally noticed that of recent years the large unit in business has had a considerable advantage over the small, and that even those small employers who survive have tended to become directly or indirectly dependent on greater concerns. The second is what is conveniently called the *exploitation* of the workers. That the workers of the world do not get returned to them—let alone the *full* product of their labour—even enough to enable them to live in reasonable comfort, and to absorb what they produce so as to keep industry running, is observable to anyone who has noted the immense productive capacity of the modern world and the complete failure of markets. The world is full of half-starved and able persons who are anxious to work, and of salesmen with warehouses packed with goods which they cannot sell to the same half-starved persons, because they are unemployed or underpaid.

These two facts are so obvious that Marxist economics are not required to prove them. From them anyone may, by any process of argument, deduce the central point of Marxist theory—the existence of a class struggle, a fact in any case illustrated whenever a strike occurs. The *existence* of such a struggle is all that we need to assume. We need not assume, as so many discussions of Marxism do, that the class struggle is a desirable or pleasing phenomenon, or that we are in a position to predict which side will be victorious.

This rejection of the superstructure of Marxist economics as superfluous has in fact been made by serious revolutionary students for some time past. It is over ten years now since Karl Radek, the famous Bolshevik theorist, silenced and shocked a British Communist objector at a Third International Congress. " Surplus value ? " he said, picking up his interrupter's words, " surplus value ? What is that ? I seem to have heard about it at school."[1]

But the theory of historical materialism cannot be treated so cavalierly. In the first place, it has commanded a far greater measure of universal acceptance than the other two principles we have mentioned. The dialectic has been adopted by no philosophers and few if any scientists outside Russia. The theory of surplus value is widely disputed, and rarely used as an explanation of current economic problems. But every historical text-book that is less than twenty years old bears plain marks of the influence of the theory of historical materialism. The old-fashioned history-book, which explained history either in terms of a conflict of ideas or as the story of a succession of great men, is far less popular than it used to be. Its place has largely been taken by a new type of book, which studies attentively economic and social conditions, and interprets the story that it has to tell in the light of these.

At the risk of tediousness, it is worth while quoting in full Marx's own summary of his theory. It is to be

[1] If any reader thinks that I have too summarily dismissed these important parts of Marxism, I would ask him to refer to my book on *Karl Marx* for a fuller analysis.

found in the Preface to his *Critique of Political Economy*, and runs as follows:

" The general conclusion at which I arrived and which, once reached, continued to serve as the leading thread in my studies, may be briefly summed up as follows: In the social production which men carry on they enter into definite relations that are indispensable and independent of their will; these relations of production correspond to a definite state of development of their material powers of production. The sum total of these relations of production constitutes the economic structure of society—the real foundation, on which rise legal and political superstructures and to which correspond definite forms of social consciousness. The mode of production in material life determines the general character of the social, political and spiritual processes of life. It is not the consciousness of men that determines their existence, but, on the contrary, their social existence determines their consciousness. At a certain stage of their development, the material forces of production in society come in conflict with the existing relations of production, or—what is but a legal expression for the same thing—with the property relations within which they had been at work before. From forms of development of the forces of production these relations turn into their fetters. Then comes the period of social revolution. With the change of the economic foundation the entire immense superstructure is more or less rapidly transformed. In considering such transformations the distinction should always be made between the material transformation of the economic conditions of production which can be determined with the precision of natural science, and the legal, political, religious, æsthetic or philosophic—in short ideological forms in which men become conscious of this conflict and fight it out. Just as our opinion of an individual is not based on what he thinks of himself, so can we not judge of such a period of transformation by its own consciousness; on the contrary, this consciousness must rather be explained from the contradictions of material life, from the existing conflict between the social forces of production and the relations of production. No social order ever disappears before all the productive forces, for which there is room in it, have been developed; and new higher relations of production never appear before the material conditions of their existence have matured in the womb of the old society. Therefore, mankind always takes up only such problems as it can solve; since, looking at the matter more closely, we will always find that the problem itself arises only when the material conditions necessary for its solution already exist or are at least in the process of formation. In broad outlines we can designate the Asiatic, the ancient, the feudal, and the modern bourgeois methods of production as so many epochs in the progress of the economic formation of society. The bourgeois relations of production are the last antagonistic form, not in the sense of individual antagonism, but of one arising from conditions of the life of individuals in society; at the same time the productive forces developing in the womb of bourgeois society create the material conditions for the solution of that antagonism. This social formation constitutes, therefore, the closing chapter of the prehistoric stage of human society.''

The theory is called materialism, a philosophic name, because it is philosophically contrasted with idealism. The idealists among historians regard history as controlled by ideas—whether those be advanced ideas such as the idea of freedom which inspired the French in 1789 or the Americans in 1776, or the less enlightened religious fury which directed the armies of the Caliph Omar. They regard the ideas, that is to say, not the material conditions of mankind, as the real energizing and directing forces in history. The Marxist materialist considers this belief is the exact opposite of the facts. It is common sense stood upon its head. The Marxist believes that it is the material circumstances of mankind that produce and condition the ideas current in society. No sane Marxist— as Engels agreed in his *Feuerbach*—would deny that the political ideas thus produced and conditioned acquire power of their own. They may hold up the natural evolution of society for some time; they may advance it and save suffering and convulsions. Nevertheless, they remain the children of economic circumstances. Out of date, they cannot withstand for ever economic evolution. They will be eaten away and collapse. Advanced, they cannot live if they are too far ahead of the evolution of society. Attempts may be made to apply them, but they will end in pathetic failures, as did all Robert Owen's gallant " Projects for a Community."

This distinction is not merely a distinction of the study, of importance for professors of history but for no others. It affects the day-to-day propaganda of any advocate of social change. The idealist in the philosophical sense—who is very often also the idealist in the conversational sense—devotes his attention to argument and emotional appeal calculated to change the ideas to which he objects. He thinks that by so doing he is attacking social oppression at its roots. The Marxist, on the other hand, considers not justice but power. He reckons what are the chief forces in society to-day, what are their interests and how they can be appealed to. Demands for " a change of heart," so frequently made by Labour parties and Christian reform parties in English-speaking countries, he does not (if he is orthodox) regard as absolutely ineffective. But he considers that they can only be effective against ideals which are already marked down by economic circumstances for death. When ideas are no longer viable, they are due victims for emotional oratory: when circumstances have changed so that their chances of life are lowered, then and then alone can propaganda hasten their death. Artificial methods of reducing fertility, for example, were studied at the beginning of last century—indeed the pessary was known to the ancient Greeks. The suffering caused to women by excessive child-bearing was as obvious and as heartrending then as now. But the world remained entirely indifferent to this oppression of the female sex until the turn of last century, when it became clear in Western countries that unlimited fertility was no longer an advantage to capitalist economics and was indeed becoming a danger.

Improvement in sanitation had removed the check of infantile mortality, and the mechanization of industry had curtailed the ability of industry to absorb an ever-increasing army of workers. Only then was the knowledge of contraceptives spread far and wide by earnest propagandists, who for the first time secured sympathetic hearing and large subscriptions instead of unnoticed sentences of imprisonment. Justice and humanity were their arguments, and were no doubt the genuine motives of the chief propagandists. But eternal though these verities are, they were only bowed to when it became economically profitable to do so. " Only in action," said Marx, meditating on a somewhat parallel phenomenon, "do there come great changes of consciousness."

In the description of the theory of historical materialism, one error is very commonly made. It is frequently assumed that Marxism regards economic circumstances as the only real agent of change, the only *causa causans* in history. The alternative description of the theory as " economic de_erminism " assists in this belief, and common sense revolts from it. Men observe that racial differences exist, and that these by general consent affect men's behaviour. They also notice that geographical circumstances greatly influence human history. Economic development is by no means the only thing that explains the differences between a desert Arab and the average inhabitant of Wisconsin. Personal differences, due to hereditary influences or education, also require explanation.

These objections are not captious; Marxist expositions which ignore them (and there have been some) are unsatisfactory. Nevertheless, such expositions are not orthodox; or, if they be orthodox, so much the worse for orthodoxy. Orthodox Marxism is in that case useless to practical revolutionaries and some form of mild heresy must be preferred to it. For the only form in which Marxist historical materialism is acceptable is in a form which states that economic conditions are the *most frequent* agents of change. They, compared with others, are more subject to rapid alteration; they are consequently the most frequent agents of social change. No doubt the English social system would be greatly changed if in the next few years the British Isles were rapidly repopulated by negroes. But there is no probability of such a drastic racial change either there or anywhere else in the world. No doubt also the history of the United States would be drastically affected if Saharan aridity spread out from Arizona all across the continent. But there is no likelihood of such a geographical change suddenly turning the Americans into Bedouins. Nor, finally, is it possible to estimate the effects of education and heredity on individuals. We can only say that, by rule of thumb, there appears to be a fairly constant ratio in all classes of feeble-minded, of thugs, of honest men, of sadists and of geniuses; or, if there is not, that no means have yet been found of estimating either the variation or its causes.

It must, however, be admitted that there is one great dark patch in the theory of historical materialism. We may accept the objective truth of the Marxist position. History appears to be in fact intelligibly interpreted as a struggle of classes. Classes do appear to act—in mass, and with individuals in all classes acting eccentrically—in accordance with their economic interests, and to hold ideas which are economically profitable to them. But it has never yet been satisfactorily explained how this alchemy works in the individual mind. How does the class interest, in each man's thoughts, wrap itself up in the garments of Justice and Right ? That it does so, there is no doubt. It is, quite probably, to the interest of the proletariat as a whole that there should be a militant Socialist movement. But it is not to the individual interest of any one of the devoted and long-suffering propagandists who keep the Socialist and Trade Union movements alive. Almost any one of them could have done better for himself by turning his talents and energy to his personal advancement. But Socialism, the interest of the proletariat, has assumed for him the appearance of eternal truth, and he can do no other than struggle on its behalf.

The same is true of his antagonists. He is willing, often, to die for his class-interest; they are always willing to live for it, and for no more ignoble motives. Most of all is this true of the clergy. They are supposed to propagate the views of a pacifist Jewish preacher, with strong tendencies towards Communism. They are placed in circumstances in which their interests should cause them to support a form of nationalist capitalism. The vast majority of them contrive, in English-speaking countries at least, to prefer the second choice. But to assume that they are consciously dishonest is obviously absurd to anyone who knows them. War and usury, to the late Archbishop of Armagh, had successfully assumed the appearance of Christianity. The fact is undeniable; it is only the mechanics of the substitution which is open to investigation.

Nevertheless, whatever be the explanation of this psychological curiosity, if the fact is admitted the practical revolutionary can base his policy upon it.

The practical deductions which the serious student draws are not many, but they are of the first importance. Marxist theory, if it is accepted, shows revolution as a comprehensible process, as a semi-predictable development. It does not indeed permit us (despite Marx's own words) to prophesy that there *will* be a revolution; but it does permit us to say that *if* there is a revolution only one class can provide the main motive force. That is, the working class. The historical development of society which Marx outlined suggests that the feudal noble, the bourgeois, and the proletarian each in turn and for comprehensible reasons become the ruling class. If we accept this a practical consequence follows. We, as reformers, or revolutionaries, must judge the organizations to which we belong and to which we pay subscriptions by a new criterion. We must not ask ourselves: " Are the objects of this body, as outlined in its rules, such that I can approve of it ? " We must ask ourselves: " Does this body command sufficient support among the only potentially revolutionary class—the workers—to justify us in spending time or money on it ? If not, does it by its programme and personnel have the potentiality of acquiring a predominant influence upon the workers ? " If the answer to both these questions is " No "; then every serious advocate of social change will withhold his support; or, if he sends a subscription, will realize that he does so only as a private indulgence of some sentimental weakness of his own.

The history of revolutionary change in the last century and a half appears to bear out the Marxian hypothesis. This aspect of history is very little studied, as yet, in English-speaking countries. More investigation, it is true, has been made of it in the last ten years than ever before; but the economic and class aspect of history since, say, 1789 is still far from widely known. If I might summarize briefly here the result of many years' study, I should say that the development of revolution is marked in Europe by four essential dates: 1789, 1848, 1871, 1917: and that the changes marked by these dates strongly reinforce the arguments for the correctness of the orthodox Marxist argument.

In 1789, in France, we find a revolution whose effects were in a fairly short space of time spread all over the then civilized world. Stripped of the unimportant but spectacular accretions—the new calendar, the Republican machinery, the religion of Theophilanthropy—we find that the revolution's abiding work was to destroy the noble class and the

C

feudal law of property. The division of mankind into castes was abolished and the right of the nobility to control the land (" no land without a *seigneur* " was once a legal axiom), and the machinery of government, and to make the laws, was destroyed. At the same time, the noble families lost the greater portion of their wealth and had reluctantly to take their place among the commoners around them. Wealth and political power were henceforward to be acquired by trade and manufacture. Careers were open to all, and circumstances were now favourable to the growth of industrial society as we see it to-day.

It seems no misuse of terms to describe this as " a bourgeois revolution."

During times of revolution society passes swiftly, in a few years, through phases which otherwise would occupy it a very long time. And, not unnaturally, in these periods of febrile development, some of the more far-sighted revolutionaries have a glimpse of developments that cannot in fact occur till generations have passed. So during the " bourgeois " French revolution there were a few eccentric and slightly demented characters who perceived that behind the victorious bourgeoisie was appearing a class—hardly as yet crystallized, certainly not conscious of itself— which would in its turn attempt to oust the then victorious class. They declared, with an almost uncanny perceptiveness, that the new-found political liberty would leave a great labouring population, in town and country, subjected to economic subjection and misery. At the height of the Jacobin dictatorship, in 1793 and 1794, unskilled attempts were made to prevent this by price laws and sumptuary regulations, and in 1796 an elaborate and fantastic plot for a communist society, directed by François Noel Babeuf, advanced to the point of organizing an unsuccessful insurrection.

The revolutions of 1848, for those who seek for drama, are uninteresting. " History does repeat itself—once as tragedy and once as farce " was said of that year. The events are ludicrous and the chief actors are contemptible. But for those who regard revolutionary movements not as an outlet for their own emotions but as subjects for laboratory study, the 1848 revolutions are as passionately interesting as a hermaphrodite, as a maturing tadpole, or as any exhibit which lies halfway between one form of life and another. The revolutions of 1848 were both bourgeois and proletarian, and this double character led to a violent internal conflict and to their speedy death. They have but little immediate importance in history: they are merely preserved for our study, like fœtuses or monsters in glass jars.

The revolutions of 1848 occurred in London (abortive wholly), Paris, Frankfurt, Berlin, Vienna, Budapest, Milan, Turin and Rome. The first dramatically successful blow was struck in Paris in February, and within a few weeks successes followed in all the chief European capitals. The pullulating minor royalties of that generation granted constitutions enthusiastically or whiningly according to their temperaments. Before the year was out, after a series of ignoble and confused disturbances, these constitutions had been withdrawn.

The reasons for this collapse are to be seen most clearly in Paris, the city whose fate decided the fate of all other revolutionary movements. The revolution of February 1848 put into power a government which consisted chiefly of orthodox republicans. There were two members of it who called themselves social revolutionaries—Louis Blanc, a journalist, and a gasworker named Albert. If Albert had any other name, history has not recorded it: he signed government decrees " Albert, *ouvrier*," and confined his political activities to a gaping admiration of his journalistic colleague. These two men found outside the government an enthusiastic revolutionary force pressing them on. They were adjured, in terms of passionate admiration and affection, to bring about the social equality that they preached, by means which neither they nor their supporters conceived at all clearly. As soon as this demand became articulate, the revolutionary forces that had driven out the King split into two. Momentarily, across Europe, the three classes in society, typifying three phases of history, could be seen, isolated and separated, frozen by a Medusa's head. The royal-landed-noble class, recently and suddenly deprived of political power; the bourgeois—trading and manufacturing class— which till now had been the source of all change in thought and in industry; and the working class, now first making an uncertain appearance in history as a conscious class.

The moment of suspense did not last long. The bourgeoisie in every country turned quickly to the landed nobility that it had so recently fought, and in alliance with it drove the new and menacing class back to where it belonged. Louis Blanc and Albert, *ouvrier*, lost their positions and before long, for greater safety, the moderate republicans were replaced by Napoleon III. In all European countries a tacit *alliance cordiale* was made between the Liberal bourgeoisie and the Tory squirearchy. Sometimes, as in France, where the nobility had been ground to powder, there were very few relics of feudalism. Elsewhere, as in Germany, the nobility retained a formidable array of privileges.

Nothing, then, was left to come in the way of revolutions after this alliance had been cemented but a rising of the proletariat alone. In 1871, when the French bourgeoisie was momentarily shattered to pieces by the German victory, the Paris Commune held power for two months. It was a working-class revolutionary body: and it is honoured in history for that and for no other reason, for it lacked both intelligence and courage. All that became it in its short life was the way in which it left it: at the end it fought desperately, and tens of thousands died for it.

Half a century later, in Russia in 1917, the Russian workers carried out a successful proletarian revolution. The town workers, directed by an *élite* to whom even their opponents would not deny skill, courage and obstinacy, founded and carried to victory the

Soviet Republic. This was done with the tacit or open acquiescence of the peasantry.

Here is the story of the last century and a half, from a Marxist viewpoint.

If we accept this view of an ordered progress in history, we still must observe that Marxism gives us but little guidance about the mechanics of revolution. The mere realization that the working class was the most probable instrument of revolution seemed to many Socialists—as a study of the debates of the Second International will show—a sufficient indication. They felt that they had only to organize within their ranks an adequate number of working men for the revolution to be achieved. How erroneous this was the German Social Democrats showed in 1918.

Moreover, the picture of past history as a regular process, from feudal noble through bourgeois society to proletarian, had a peculiar effect on the minds of those who accepted it. By a common error, an *ordered* progress was assumed in the student's mind to be an *inevitable* progress. Because certain past events had proceeded in an order which fell into a certain pattern, orthodox Marxists assumed (and many still assume) that future events would necessarily continue and conclude that pattern. As soon as that assumption is stated, its absurdity is apparent: nevertheless, the inevitability of a victorious proletarian revolution is proclaimed habitually both in Marxist text-books and Communist propaganda. Yet the validity of such a prophecy has never been investigated, and indeed is probably by its nature incapable of being investigated. It is at least possible, to use no stronger phrase, that our present economic difficulties may end in some other solution than a victorious Communist revolution—Fascism, for example, or the destruction of all ordered town life by a new war.

What we may for the moment regard as proved is perhaps no more than this: the continual increase of class from which a revolutionary urge may be expected. Also, Marxist economics suggest that at the same time the structure of capitalism will be continually shaken by slumps. But even here the realistic revolutionary will enter a caveat. Marxist prophecy has failed in part. The industrial working class has indeed increased in numbers, but the capitalist class has not decreased correspondingly. It was hoped originally that as capital units grew bigger and bigger and small businesses were eaten up, a tiny group of employers would be faced with a vast mass of expropriated workers. A struggle would follow, whose results might be predicted with some confidence. The oppressors would soon have but one throat to be cut. " Nero grinned," wrote Marx in his famous manifesto, " when he found that all Africa was owned by only five landowners."

But the workers to-day have no opportunity to grin like Neros. Joint-stock companies, which had only recently become legal when Marx's manifesto was written, have preserved the great middle class from extinction. The man who once would have run a small business now holds shares in a great one—

possibly in several. The class of shareholders and rentiers is functionless indeed, but it is great in number. And if the shareholders are economically powerless (as they are, for what business to-day is really run by its shareholders ?) they are not politically powerless. Both as voters and as the rank and file of " patriotic " associations of Fascists, the middle class can at crucial moments wield great political power. The great division remains; the employers face the working men; the class struggle goes on. But the battlefield is obscured and tactics made more complicated by a horde of functionless or almost functionless camp followers, who tend, by tradition and financial interest, to attach themselves to the employer's side.

It would be, however, a grave mistake to assume that the whole of the middle class was " functionless "—that it consisted wholly of people who drew dividends and pottered in suburban shops. Many of them are more properly classed as " technicians." By superior education and sometimes by superior ability they hold the bigger managerial and technical posts, and they work for their living as regularly and inevitably as the most horny-handed of us. But their training and their wage-scales put them in the ranks of the middle class; although they are by no means so naturally the enemies of the revolution as are their coupon-clipping colleagues.

Analysis on Marxist lines of these sub-classes that uneasily fringe the two great classes is by no means easy. It does not, however, invalidate our main conclusion, which is that the chief force of change, the chief agent of revolution, must be proletarian. As a corollary of that, human suspicions being what they are, it must be admitted that the controlling individuals, the general staff of the revolution, must if they are to secure the allegiance of their followers be mostly proletarian in origin. This does not, obviously, forbid the use of non-proletarians of eminent qualities in key positions—a rule which would have excluded both Marx and Lenin but neither Mussolini nor Hitler from working-class leadership—but it does require us to view with suspicion allegedly revolutionary bodies whose directors are chiefly middle class or upper class. There are individuals in every class who do not follow their class direction. There are aristocratic revolutionaries and conservative working men. But, watched over a period of time and considered in broad outlines, classes are seen to move as unitary bodies in pursuit of their own interests.

What was added to this, by Marxist interpreters, was before Lenin almost wholly in the nature of footnotes and elaborate explanations of the obvious. The chief commentators were German, and they carried into economics the methods which characterized the last stage of German classical scholarship. They passionately desired an authority; independence of thought was their chief terror. They established the text of the master's words with loving meticulousness: when they had secured the perfect exemplar, they polished it till it shone. Everything that was obvious they commented upon with delighted verbosity. Whatever was difficult or practical they passed by in silence. The theory of the dictatorship of the proletariat, for example, one of the least clear and most important parts of Marxist theory, they left almost wholly without comment. Occasionally they would quote aphorisms for or against Parliamentarism—such as Marx's remark that a revolution might occur in constitutional forms in England and Holland alone, or Engels's that the bourgeoisie was being " killed by legal activity " (*la légalite nous tue*)—but a serious study they evaded as nervously as Herr Vollmer evaded a genuine difficulty in a classical text. Almost the only book, indeed, which honestly faced the problem was a frankly anti-revolutionary book by Eduard Bernstein, *Evolutionary Socialism*, and the shrill rage with which it was greeted was not so much the indignation of the genuine revolutionary as the vexation of the scholar disturbed by reality.

In revenge, perhaps, they abounded in commentaries upon the more elaborate extensions of the theory of surplus value, and the correct philosophical deductions to be drawn from the developed system of the dialectic. Their excursuses in the second theme have been deprived of most of their value by the rise of psychology, a branch of study non-existent in Marx's day: in the first field their work has been equally generally forgotten with the modification of the economic conditions which gave rise to the theory of surplus value itself.

As a result, the only elaborations of the Marxist theory in the sphere of revolutionary technique are chiefly certain comments-by-the-way which occur in Marxist *historical* studies. Hyndman, for example, commented that the history of the Paris Commune showed that any Socialist government of the future should make its first act the seizure of the Bank of France, or the equivalent controlling bank in whatever country it might be. (Even this deduction passed unnoticed: Socialist and Labour governments have taken office in Western countries several times and, outside Russia, not one has laid its hands on the banking system.)

It was also observed that certain conditions of the labour market were favourable to revolutionary sentiment, and others not. The scattered comments on this phenomenon do not seem to have been ever co-ordinated; but the result of a rough survey of the facts seems to be that revolutionary sentiment reaches its peak when the condition of the working class, economically, is going sharply up or sharply down. That is to say, the " revolutionary urge " increases either when a steady rise in the standard of living is sharply checked and turned into a painful and obvious decline; or when a gradual rise in the standard of living comes after a period of great discomfort. In the latter case the working man has recent memories of suffering and a small increase in comfort and leisure gives him energy and strength to express his resentment. The history of the Chartist Movement in Great Britain shows the latter process working with almost thermometrical exactitude. The General Strike of 1842 was directly caused by a sudden and harsh trade crisis, of the usual Victorian kind, which brought savage suffering to the workers immediately after a more peaceful and easy period in which the bad conditions of earlier years had seemed to be slowly improving. The hysterical and helpless outburst of 1848, the last spasm of Chartism, came two years after the great misery and famine of 1846. The hideous wretchedness of that year was over, and the working class was at once sore from its wounds and yet sufficiently recovered to think it had strength enough to seek its revenge.

A similar cycle may perhaps be observed in the latest history of British industrial convulsions. Twice, since the war, the British trade unions have taken action which seemed menacing to the governing class. The years 1921 and 1922, especially the latter, were filled with the noise of big strikes and lock-outs —miners, engineers and others—and continuous and angry disorder by the unemployed. The least intelligent observer noticed that these were due to the sudden commercial crash and the consequent sharp worsening of conditions which was forced upon a once-prosperous working class. Again, in 1926, with the General Strike, British labour delivered the heaviest single blow ever struck against a Western capitalist government. At first sight, such a resurgence of energy seems to be an exception to the rule. But in fact it is not: the attack was delivered after the British unions had had a couple of years to recover from the great depression. A careful study, such as G. D. H. Cole's *Guide through World Chaos*, shows somewhat unexpectedly that the figures for the two years preceding the great strike indicate a definite improvement in working-class conditions.

From this we may deduce—what in any case seems confirmed by common sense—that neither a steadily prosperous nor a hopelessly degraded working class is a reliable revolutionary force. A steadily prosperous proletariat, like the American workers who filled the ranks of the American Federation of Labour during the long reign of Samuel Gompers, has no interest in revolutionary theories, however turbulent the habits of individual members may be. A grossly oppressed working class, without hope, may riot, but it will do no more. The *Lumpen-proletariat*, the proletariat broken down to slum conditions, has neither the energy nor the cohesion to take part in a revolution. It may, as in Bavaria in 1919, momentarily support a revolution only to desert it ficklely at the first check. It may, as when Cavaignac armed it in Paris in 1848, take arms for a few pence to crush the very revolutionaries who are fighting in its defence.

A further deduction from Marxist principles is one which has been admitted in theory by most Socialist parties and denied in practice by all. It is argued that the essential theories of Marxism prove the impossibility of a Socialist revolution by parliamentary and constitutional means. The moment you admit the general validity of the theory of the class struggle in history, democracy is seen to be an unusable instrument. Only the most elementary political thinking is satisfied with the remark " the workers are the vast majority; therefore they must win under democracy."

If it is agreed that in general, classes and groups vote and act in accordance with their immediate interests—and indeed daily experience suggests that that is true—then it is probable that there is a probable majority in every country (no matter how industrialized) *against* a revolutionary Socialist change. For it is not the fact that a majority of the population would find such a change to its immediate interest. It is the grossest self-delusion for the " advanced " thinker to neglect this truth. Let us examine the question class by class. That the employing class may be expected to be in opposition we can all agree. To them must be added the large rentier class: the inhabitants of the suburban ring of every large city. But further there must be added to them the workers in every form of luxury and semi-luxury trades which are dependent upon the continued existence of a capitalist class. It is not only the painter, R.A., A.R.A., or only would-be R.A., who is either a reactionary or declares that art is supreme and requires the artist to take no interest in politics. The same attitude (less elegantly expressed) is taken up by waiters and gentlemen's gentlemen. It is within the knowledge of every trade union official that such trades as clerking and shopkeeping are very nearly unorganizable. Those who are employed in them have proletarian wages, proletarian conditions and often proletarian appearance, but they have not proletarian minds. Consciously, or sub-consciously, they are aware that their livelihood depends upon the continued existence of a moneyed class; therefore, unless they have the hope and intention of changing their occupation, they either have no political opinions at all, or political opinions compatible with the retaining of their customers' privileged position.

This may seem a highly theoretical argument, but it will be found to be a very practical one in everyday life. Almost any Labour agent or Socialist political official is aware of it, and bears it in mind. Only the rawest recruit to modern political agitation imagines that the working class is " the great majority " and therefore an electoral programme with a purely proletarian appeal will bring a victory. The experienced agent will tell you at once that what holds the balance is a floating mass which is vaguely called " middle-class opinion." In Great Britain, for example, a most highly industrialized country, there are out of over 600 only some 200 Parliamentary seats that can be probably won by the proletarian vote, and of these half at most can be regarded as " safe Labour seats." The rest depend upon this vote which is commonly called middle-class or suburban: it may be semi-proletarianized, as in Acton or Fulham, or highly conscious of its respectability, as in Brighton, Ealing or Hendon. To conciliate this vote is essential to the gaining of a majority, and it is significant that a skilled politician rarely suggests that it can be conciliated by any other method than by " moderating the more extreme parts of our programme," or, more specifically, " soft-pedalling Socialism."

This is not an accident due to a freak of an electoral system, or to a chance arrangement of constituencies. Wherever a Socialist party has approached near to office in an advanced industrial country the same thing has happened—in Italy, Germany, France and Britain. In each country the party has progressed a certain way with a genuinely Socialist or revolu-tionary programme, only to find that its further progress depended on a gradual abandonment of that programme. Sometimes, as in Germany, this abandonment took place fairly consistently, to the growing exasperation of the proletarian and revolu-tionary core which had set the party out on its career. Sometimes, as in France, efforts were made to keep the party to the logical strictness of its pro-gramme, and the more realist politicians, Briands, Vivianis, Millerands, dropped the unadorned Socialist label for some more qualified, hyphenated label which would be found electorally more appeal-ing. In every case the result seemed to be the same, a purely Socialist, constitutionally-revolutionary pro-gramme will carry you a certain way and then come to a dead stop. The maximum number of seats obtainable so seems to be, at a rough estimate, about one-third of the total.[1]

[1] Perhaps I may be allowed a word of personal explanation here. This argument, or a similar one, was advanced by me in 1920 in my

In theory this argument appears irresistible. It has appeared irresistible to the author of this book, and under its influence he joined the Communist Party and became editor of its official organ. When it became clear, even to his affectionate eyes, that in no probable or even conceivable circumstances could the British Communist (or any other party) direct or attempt a violent and unconstitutional British revolution, he withdrew from the Communist Party, and was inclined to the belief that all attempts at radical political change were henceforward doomed to frustration.

But it appears to the writer now—and he is fully conscious that in putting forward this view he may be as much misled by his unconscious desires as the worst of those he has criticized—that the argument is not universally true. It appears untrue in certain circumstances, and these circumstances are likely to be found before long in England and not improbably in America as well.

Observe that the validity of the argument depends upon the classes in consideration having certain well-defined interests, and on those interests being fairly easily apprehensible. If a time comes when any large body is wholly uncertain of its interests and at the same time is being driven to desperation by great or unexpected suffering, then it becomes no longer an

book *The Bolshevik Theory* and was endorsed, I was flattered to know, by V. I. Lenin, who commented in very complimentary terms on the book at the time. The exception (if it can be called such) which I make here was not made then, and to that extent I have modified my views.

D

obstacle to change, but an addition to the force of any group which is sufficiently powerful to impress its will upon it, to dominate it, and to use its strength to its own ends. In such a condition the members of the distracted class are not cohesive and have no power of directing themselves; they are, as Trotsky called the Nazis, human dust.

Such a fate, in part or wholly, has at times overtaken the middle class in Western Europe. Both in Italy and in Germany its confidence in the future was shattered and it floundered from Left to Right in ever-increasing hysteria. The more realist Socialists of Italy and Germany will admit, to-day, that the Socialist parties of those two countries had their opportunity to make a Socialist revolution; that they failed to take it and for that reason are extinct. In 1920, about the peak time of the Italian revolutionary upheaval, when the walls were covered with *VV Lenin*, the Italian middle class was resigned to its fate. Dissensions within the working-class ranks continually adjourned the time of the revolution, until, distracted beyond endurance by continually deferred doom, the middle class threw itself behind a sort of Prætorian Guard.

In Germany, too, in the last act of the funeral of the Social-Democratic Party, the session of the Reichstag in the Potsdam Chapel which granted Hitler his extraordinary powers, a most significant scene took place. Otto Wels, the elderly Social-Democratic leader, delivered, not without courage, a speech on what he described as the reforms demanded by the working class. Hitler answered in a phrase whose exact words are disputed, but whose effect was: " This is all very well-sounding. But why have you never done any of these things ? You have had the power to, and you have not done them." To that there was not, and could not be, an answer.

In such a time, it is clear, only firm and adventurous leadership can enable a revolutionary party to take control. Tactics which once appealed to middle-class voters—tactics of respectability and moderation —suddenly cease to appeal; only speeches and acts which suggest rapid and decisive steps (to an end which may well be quite imperfectly apprehended) are attractive. But politicians, even nominally revolutionary politicians, are generally far too fixed in their minds and habits to make so rapid a change. There is frequently a swing, at such times, of disillusioned and clamorous " petty bourgeois " to the Left Wing parties, because the disillusioned ones have for so long accepted as true the picture that their journals have drawn of these parties. They have read so often—once with terror, now with hope—of the Labour Party or Socialist Party as grimly intent on hasty, painful and drastic change. But the respectable reality rapidly disgusts them, and they become fit material for men who are really no more than private adventurers—mixtures of gangster and of company promoter, such as is the most effective Fascist leader.

That this picture is overdrawn and unlovable is probably true. It is not fair to charge all the middle class, even in the process of being ground to pieces in the present crisis of capitalism, with being frantic and brainless in its behaviour. Hysteria is the directing power of Surbiton and Hoover Heights, it is true, but there are many technicians and professional men who cannot fairly be classed with the vapid and parasitic livers-off-coupons and chief-clerks-in-offices. Many of them, finding how regularly the operation of the competitive system checks them in their task and prevents the full use of the discoveries they are expected to make and the resources they are supposed to organize, have a strong theoretical sympathy for Socialism or Communism. But even here the result is the same. They come—and what Socialist has not seen this frequently occur in the past few years ?—to the existing ostensible revolutionary party, expecting that it will have a plan for the reconditioning of society and a use for their services. They find nothing whatever—for a number of electoral devices and a collection of pre-war pamphlets which is nearly all that the parties outside the Communist International possess, is nothing—and, vexed and disillusioned turn themselves to support some Mosley, Mussolini, Hitler, or Bottomley who will present them with at least the *simulacrum* of intelligent and confident direction.

In such a time a sure and drastically minded revolutionary Socialist Party can command success: if it is hesitant and formalist it will be precipitated into bloody ruin. Such a time is planning-time or Hitler-time; it depends on ourselves which it is.

If we are discussing methods of drastic social change we cannot stop at this point. We may dislike the phenomenon which is called Fascism, but that is no reason for refraining from investigating it. The true scientific investigator rejoices as much in a pus-filled ulcer as in a red dawn, and may well derive more enlightenment from the former.

Unfortunately, there is but little written material about Fascist methods of revolution. Investigation on the spot is difficult, for many reasons, and the material uncovered is but little help for our present purpose, though priceless to a student of criminal pathology. It is better printed in an appendix to books like those of Krafft-Ebing than in a manual of political change.

The sole book pretending to deal with Fascist methods is by a certain Signor Curzio Malaparte, called *The Technique of the Coup d'État*. It contains, upon investigation, three types of material, as follows: (1) A considerable deal of anecdotes concerning revolutionary moments at which the author was present, and showed superhuman penetration. (2) A little chop-licking recollection of what he and his friends did to the Italians who were ill-advised enough to belong to the working class in Florence and elsewhere. (3) An observation—in itself quite true—that Trotsky has shown that in a *coup d'état* it is more important to strike at railway stations, telegraph exchanges, pumping stations, etc., than at the formal centres of power—town halls, ministries and so forth.

This does not get us much farther.

But if the Fascist Movement has not much to say for itself, it does not follow that Marxist methods may not enable us to extract something of value from a study of it despite itself. The Fascist régime, as we have said, is a prætorian, a janissary régime. But no Prætorian Guard, and no body of janissaries are independent of the country, the time and the class that surround them. Fascism may tyrannize, to a greater or less extent, over all classes. Nevertheless, it is itself a class movement and reflects a definite class outlook. It is petty-bourgeois.

This phrase has been used so often and so unintelligently by Marxist writers that one hesitates to use it. It, together with the word *bourgeois*, has become, for many speakers, scarcely more effective or meaning a word of abuse than another word beginning with the same letter. But in this case it has a definite meaning. We can see, as soon as we contemplate it for more than a minute, that Fascism reflects, almost mirror-like, the mentality of a broken-down middle class. All the insanities and stupidities that the outer world has such pain to understand fall together into a pattern when they are regarded as a projection on a vast screen of the contents of a suburban head. Fascism, for example, brings with it a genuine harrying of certain types of big business—especially financiers and Jews " who ruin small men," and the owners of department- and chain-stores whose places of business are successful and unwisely conspicuous. The Church, after passing through a few difficult moments while hysteria was at its height and there was still a chance of genuine revolution, is reinstated for respectability's sake. It is significant that the Roman Catholic Church, the church which is believed in the suburbs to be the most *chic* church, has up till now come to the most profitable arrangements with Fascism. Extreme and ostentatious patriotism, of the type favoured by small chambers of commerce and by suburban tennis clubs, is equally typical of the prejudices of the small bourgeoisie. From the same social root comes the passion for uniformity, which is the necessary condition of respectability. All must rise when the band plays "Giovanezza," "Horst Wessel," "God Save the King," or "My Country 'Tis of thee." All must wear the same clothes, or clothes as nearly similar as may be. Better still, all who can must get into uniform, the one attire which is considered by the lower-middle class to be always the thing. (Of course, not all uniforms will do. A commissionaire's will not do; but an O.T.C. uniform most emphatically will.)

Other spontaneous characteristics of Fascism, not apparently called for by any economic or political need, can be traced back to just this class mentality. "Higher" education is discouraged and technical education ("teaching the working class to *work*") expected to replace it: at the same time, with profound illogicality, the most snob schools and colleges —the equivalents of Eton and West Point—are adulated and encouraged, merely for their "classy" character and despite their curriculum. Similar is

the source of the violent suppression of all " in-
decency "—the forbidding of nudism, the sacking of
Dr. Hirschfeld's clinic in Berlin, the banning of all
sexual studies in Germany; the prevention of birth
control in Italy; and similar Puritanical phenomena.
In no other section of the community is sexual knowledge more feared and abhorred than in the lower-
middle class. Were it not so, perhaps the Fascists
would know why they reintroduced beating into
the schools and "discipline" everywhere, why they
reinforce the subjection of women to men, and why
their victories are always celebrated and accompanied by widespread floggings.

Everywhere Fascism is the projection on to a huge
screen of a picture dimly, dreamingly floating in
suburban brains. Mr. Browne can no longer in his
suburb be the regnant head of a family that he wishes
to be. The head of the house—the little king!
Probably his children disobey him and racket
around; even his wife may defy him. Certainly, outside his house he is ever less the potent figure he
would like to be. Most likely he is a second clerk,
terrified of losing his job, whose life is one continual
*Yes, sir* and *No, sir*; even if he is nominally independent, with his own shop or store, he knows that he is
helpless in the hands of, say, a great tobacco company.
The Fascist revolution half satisfies his unacted
desires. At least others shall do for him what he
would like to see done—drill and discipline children,
put women back to cooking Brownes' dinners and
give their jobs to Brownes, clout the cads in the

unions, make people salute the flag and support decent private schools . . . and all that.

Such a body of doctrine is nonsensical, no doubt. It is also self-destructive, in that certain portions of it are likely to lead to the explosion of a fresh great war. This does not prevent it being genuinely powerful, but it does mean that certain definite lines of policy with regard to it are enforced upon us.

The official Communist International attitude to Fascism is clearly, in view of this analysis, seen to be hopelessly and disastrously wrong. It was laid down, up to 1933, in repeated declarations in the most crabbed Marxist jargon, addressed chiefly to the German workers. It is held to some extent in circles outside the Communist Party in Great Britain. It is, briefly, as follows: " The chief enemies of the revolution are the reformist Labour Party or Social-Democratic leaders. The serious revolutionaries must direct their attacks against them, even if necessary co-operating at times with Fascists (as the German Communists did in the Berlin transport strike). Fascism is an experience which the workers must go through. It will destroy the reformist organizations and disillusion the workers. It will probably lead to a fresh war, and out of the ruins and sufferings of that war a real revolutionary upheaval will result."

Such was the policy advocated by the Communist International as the German Nazi movement grew larger every month. When the crisis came overwhelmingly near it was appalled by the results of its own argument. Theories that had seemed perfect in the study of Bukharin were intolerable when in fact they assumed the monstrous shape of Hitler. Reversing policy suddenly, in frantic and justified alarm, the Presidium of the International on March 5th, 1933, decided that at all costs the victory of Fascism must be prevented. It called off its attack upon the " real enemies of the workers," and addressed an urgent appeal for unity to the Social Democrats, even promising to refrain from criticism of the Social Democratic leaders. But it was too late; before unity could be achieved, both Communism and Social-Democracy went down in a common ruin.

Thereafter, returning to its original attitude with a defiance of common sense which had something sublime about it, the International, with Hitler finally victorious, issued a final statement: " The policy of the (German) Central Committee with Thälmann at its head has been completely correct." It is a pity that so many of the Committee and its followers had by then been killed by the Fascists and were unable to be consoled by reading this.

It was only at the very moment of death that the German Communist movement knew the truth. But we can see at our leisure that the argument that Fascism must be allowed or aided as a probably necessary stage in revolution is one that never could have been valid. It is in itself no more than a hypothesis, a complicated weaving of what at the best can be no more than one probability upon another. For this hypothesis it would be singularly unwise to contemplate permitting the annihilation, not only of all Labour organizations, but of most of what we have been accustomed to regard as intelligent thought and personal liberty.

But even as an hypothesis this policy is hardly plausible. Fascism, it is said, will lead to a new war, and a new war will lead to a Communist revolution. But in fact it is by no means probable that war would lead to Communist revolution. Let us consider. It is hardly likely that any war could be more extensive than the last war. Yet that war led to a successful workers' revolution in one country alone, of all the score or more states involved. Nor was this one revolution in any way inevitable. At no time was it certain that the Russian Revolution would win through to victory. " We may be driven out," said Trotsky, its military leader, " but we will bang the door so that it will re-echo through history." Banging the door or not, it is clear he contemplated defeat. It was perfectly possible, at almost any moment, that the faint red flicker in Moscow would be extinguished and Russia be divided up into agrarian principalities under Koltchaks, Yudenitches, Denikins and Petluras—larger editions of slum states like Lithuania and Latvia. It is true that the conditions for the Russians would then have been, in the usual phrase, intolerable. But it is an elementary mistake in politics to imagine that because conditions are intolerable, people will not tolerate them. If force is in other hands, they will tolerate them; if they cannot tolerate them they just die. Socialists and reformers do not know that simple fact; but Nazis and White Russians do.

We are, however, treating this policy too gently in assuming that the effects of another war—so lightly contemplated by official Communist propaganda—will be in any way similar to those of the late war, little as that was in the end favourable to revolution. The results of the next war are, it is true, in part incalculable; so far as they are calculable they point to the rapid extinction of all organized society, all exchange, all ordered communication, and all the necessary media for the carrying on—let alone improvement—of human life. The power to react, to reconstruct and to organize, which the Communist thesis assumes to lie with the workers and peasants, depends on the existence of certain machinery and of certain human characteristics. Both of these will probably cease to exist.

A study of *The Probable Character of a New War* has been recently issued (by Messrs. Gollancz). Here is an extract from its description of the effects of an old-fashioned and feeble poison gas (mustard gas):

" Dichlorethyl sulphide $(CH_2ClCH_2)_2S$, known as Yellow Cross, or sometimes also as mustard gas or Yperite, is, if possible, even more mischievous in its effects. Like most other poison gases, mustard gas is not strictly speaking a gas. It is really a liquid with a high boiling-point, which has to be scattered through the air in a fine spray. Its weight causes it to fall to the ground, covering it and all the objects with which it comes in contact with an invisible and imperceptible layer. Like the bacteria of plague or cholera, or some other infectious substance which cannot be detected by the naked eye, it lies in wait for its victim, sticks to the soles or the clothing of anyone who passes, and is thus unconsciously brought into houses or dug-outs. In the warmth of a room or dug-out the poison is vaporized and mixes unnoticed with the air which is being breathed. It clings undiscovered to all living tissue, including the resistant outer skin, and after from six to eighteen hours the first symptoms begin to appear. By this time it is generally too late to give any help. The symptoms consist of necrosis of all living substances attacked by the mustard gas, such as the outer skin, the mucous membrane, the eyelids, the conjunctiva and the cornea of the eye, the bronchial tubes, the lungs, etc. This is the characteristic feature of mustard gas and can best be compared with the effects of burns. Even one part of mustard gas in five million of air can cause disease. The symptoms vary according to the nature of the tissue which is attacked. On the outer skin blisters of all sizes appear, changing rapidly to open wounds which are ready to receive all kinds of infectious bodies and are extremely difficult to heal. In the eye purulent inflammation occurs, while in the lungs considerable pieces may be eaten away on account of the extensive destruction of the bronchial walls, and the gradual exudate which ensues leads to the obstruction of the bronchiæ and alveoli by connective tissue. In other words, the bronchial tubes are slowly and progressively narrowed, and as the passage for the exchange of air becomes smaller, breathing becomes more difficult, so that the victim is gradually strangled over a period of weeks, or even months, until at last signs of suffocation appear, often accompanied by violent convulsions.

" The resorption of poison in the blood leads to equally fatal results, such as the mass destruction of the white and red blood-corpuscles, which is finally revealed on the skin by yellow or yellowish brown to bronze-coloured spots caused by the iron from the blood-corpuscles which have been destroyed (hæmosiderosis), just as after a bite from a poisonous snake the blood coagulates in the blood-vessels (thrombosis, which may cause death), and this poison leads to paralysis and convulsions in the central nervous system."

A more effective gas—though still fourteen years out of date—Lewisite, known as " Death Dew," is carried in 5-lb. gas generators, of which 500 are the full load of a commercial plane. A thousand generators can, in favourable circumstances, gas an open area of sixty square miles: two commercial planes, therefore, would be sufficient to gas London or New York.

As yet, no protection has been devised, nor is it easy to see on what lines it is to be sought. Cellars or dug-outs would have to have six-foot thick concrete roofs to withstand the ordinary bombs manufactured seven years ago; even then if they had any ventilation they would be no protection against poison gas. It is very difficult to imagine any considerable portion of a large city effectively roofed in by six feet of concrete. Any exposed portion would be liable to become a focus for the spreading effects of the light " electric incendiary bombs weighing only one kilogram. They have only to strike through a roof and then the thermite (a magnesium alloy) with which they are filled develops a heat of 3,000 degrees; the outer covering also burns and this glowing mass can eat its way even through steel. Water merely increases the incendiary effect, and no extinguishing appliance has yet been discovered. . . ."

This account could be extended indefinitely. But enough has been quoted to show the sort of picture we should have of the next war. We are not to imagine, as occurred in Paris after the Franco-Prussian war, or in Berlin in 1918, a proletariat, famished and exasperated, seizing hold of im-poverished but still intact industries and agriculture, punishing the rich who have feasted while others starved, and grimly or uncertainly, courageously or hesitantly, applying to building up a new state the les-sons of organization that their masters have taught them. We are rather to imagine a country in which, in the very first few weeks, every large town will have become a charnel-house like none that the Plague produced. Where any survive in the poison-laden, burnt and wrecked streets, half will be crippled or raving; the rest will be fighting savagely for what scraps of food can be found. In the country-side the peasants and farmers, banded together to protect their crops, will shoot at sight—when they are fortunate enough to get in first—the savage bands of town refugees roaming the country-side. Whole areas will pass out of human occupation as the winds change and the low-lying, long-waiting, heavy clouds of poison gas shift about. Where governments survive, in areas once desolate, sparsely inhabited and little considered, they will be primitive and violent organisms, like the Saxon kingdoms of the Heptarchy.

We reject, then, this theory as a possible revolutionary plan of campaign. It does not, however, exhaust what is offered as Marxist, or pseudo-Marxist, tactics. There is in existence quite a small literature about what is called " Leninism," and it is widely believed that Leninism is a new technique and theory of revolution. It is odd, therefore, to discover that in fact there is *no such thing as Leninism at all*. The " Leninist works " of Russian professors may be dismissed forthwith; the stature of these revolutionary *diadochi* is smaller than the smallest Seleucid's, but it would be most unjust to judge Lenin's works by these commentators. Lenin's own works—both his written works and his works in history—show that there is nothing new in Leninism. Leninism is only a quick and highly realist adaptation of Marxism to varying circumstances. It is ever-varying; it consists, in the end, of no more than being Lenin, of being swift, courageous, uncannily perceptive and infinitely flexible. Lenin's writings become the highest form of empiricism whenever he approaches the question of " What shall we do now ? " Where a new principle momentarily seems to appear, quite brief investigation shows it to be no more than a reflexion of external circumstances—a change in policy due to unexpected accidents and justified after the event. The Communist Party has narrow ranks and its membership is selected ? This is not a philosophical principle, but an historical incident. It is due to the fact that Tsarism for fifteen years or so saw to it that, whether the party wished it or not, the ranks of the Russian S.D.P. would be thinly filled and tenanted only by picked men, of proved intelligence and daring. No compromise in time of revolution ? That is a principle, only because during the actual revolution the Mensheviks rejected the compromise that Lenin formally offered them on September 3rd, 1917; and therefore Lenin realistically went forward on a " no compromise " basis. Every apparent principle of tactics was jettisoned instantly by Lenin, without regrets or explanations, when circumstances seemed to him to have changed, as was notably shown in his attitude to the calling of the Constituent Assembly. All Lenin's most fruitful writings—such as *The Infantile Sickness of Leftism*—are in the last analysis no more than able exhortations to his followers to abandon unrealistic behaviour and face facts.

# CHAPTER III

## SYNDICALISM, INDUSTRIAL UNIONISM

WHEREVER there is an organized movement in any country for social change it almost always has two halves. It may start as a unified body of persons with a revolutionary aim, or with merely a liking for revolutionary discussion. But as soon as it leaves the parlour and becomes a movement of large importance, it falls into halves—the political and the economic. There is always both a Party and a Trade Union organization. This is true of Socialist organizations, of Fascist organizations, of Communist organizations and even of Anarchist organizations.

The two halves do not always lie together in harmony. The tendency in most European countries has been for the political party to domineer over the trade union. This has produced, in its turn, a reaction of greater violence, in which the trade union rejected completely any alliance with a political party, and claimed that it could itself alone transform society by industrial action. " Industrial action " meant strikes, supplemented by sabotage and the boycott. The theory, which was widely known as syndicalism before the war, added that a political party was not merely superfluous: it was an actively dangerous and harmful body.

By inducing the working class to give its time and energy to political action, the political party (it was argued) took so much time and energy away from the trade unions. If political action was useless, then obviously a political party was to that extent a nuisance and a waste of energy. Energy directed to the building up of trade unions and the direction of strikes was demonstrably being used in the class struggle and could not possibly be going to waste. Energy given to contesting elections probably was.

More than that, however, the mere existence of a political party confused and misled the workers. It actually diminished their revolutionary impulse by holding out fallacious hopes to them. Whatever might be the ostensible beliefs of a Parliamentary party, it was bound in fact to tell the workers that they could change the structure of society by using their votes alone. Instead of telling them to rely upon their own strength, open or concealed, it told them effectively to appeal to the electorate's sense of justice. This, the syndicalists declared, was dangerous nonsense. What happened in fact, according to an argument already outlined in this book, was that the apparently revolutionary party had to trim its programme to suit the middle class; in other words, it had to abandon all real intention to make a drastic change.

Syndicalism first arose in France, where this argument was being continually reinforced by political history. The story of French Parliamentary Socialism before the war is one continual and ludicrous repetition of the same event. Eminent Socialist politicians rise to a certain height by announcing highly revolutionary views. They then discover that there is no conceivable chance of their taking office so long as they retain these views; they thereupon abandon them and pass shamelessly across to the other side. Viviani, the Prime Minister in 1914, had previously been a Socialist. He had abandoned his views to lead a bourgeois cabinet, which assisted in stifling an inquiry into the murder of his fellow Socialist, Jaurès. Millerand, the arch-reactionary, later expelled with great difficulty by Herriot from the Presidency, was another such. Briand is known to syndicalists not as a champion of peace, but as a one-time extreme revolutionary and advocate of the general strike, who had the unusual experience of smashing by the use of military force the very strike he had advocated.

That such a procession of betrayals was not due to a fortuitous collection of " King's bad bargains " in the French Socialist ranks seemed to be shown in 1914, when the largest of all Socialist parties showed that it had been completely infected by the same disease. The German Social-Democratic Party was Marxist and revolutionary to the last button, so far as phrases went. Moreover, the duty of a Marxist party had been laid down at an international congress and it had signified its assent in the usual manner. This duty was to seize hold of an imperialist war as an opportunity to overturn the capitalist régime.

Not a single member of the German Reichstag, nor even (so far as was known) a single member of the German Party, even thought of carrying out that instruction at the outbreak of war. The revolutionary phrases which they had uttered had, in the course of years of orderly Parliamentary agitation, ceased to have any meaning for them. They had believed that they retained the revolutionary ideas with which they joined the party, but years of unrevolutionary action had destroyed those ideas in fact. Only a hollow shell was left, and as soon as pressure was applied to it, it crumpled.

What was true of the German Party was, in a less dramatic manner perhaps, true of all parties. But the syndicalist theory did not rest exclusively upon an argument about the corrupting nature of politics. It was also historically explained by a change in the structure of trade unionism, and in its functions. Syndicalists were sometimes made by contemplation of the rogueries of politicians, it is true; but they were more often made by contemplation of the growth and change of trade unions, and by what appeared to be a legitimate conclusion as to their probable future.

This change was the substitution of industrial for craft unions. To those whose livelihood is not intimately concerned with trade union organization, this statement is probably very far from clear. It is only relatively recently, indeed, that a knowledge of trade union structure has been at all widespread among " radical " circles. There are in England and

America to-day probably quite a number still of worthy people who are convinced of the up-to-date character of their knowledge, and who believe, more or less, that there is one union for every trade, called " the Painters' Union " or " the Railwaymen's Union " or whatever it may be. " Would it were so! " the syndicalist would have replied. The trade union world is as various and tangled as a jungle. It has growths of all forms, shapes and sizes, and even (since gangsters came into the Chicago Labour world) poisonous reptiles and man-eating monsters.

But among these organizations may be traced two dominant forms. One is the craft union, the type favoured and indeed artificially preserved by the American Federation of Labour. This is the earlier form. The first trade unions were formed among workers of the same crafts, carpenters uniting with carpenters, plumbers with plumbers, compositors with compositors in an endeavour to preserve trade customs and, often enough, to exclude interlopers. Certain of these unions, when their members were exercising a well-paid and skilled craft, became rich and exclusive. They never became so rich and exclusive, nor were they able to inflict so vicious penalties on intruders, as the corresponding societies of doctors and lawyers, but they had similar isolationist and predatory tendencies.

But as their employers were neither invalids nor victims of the law, they were in due course faced with serious resistances which suggested that their course was run. The building trade employer, for example, once he had federated with his fellow employers, found himself in a highly favourable position for industrial conflict when his workers were organized in over twenty different squabbling unions. He and his fellows acted as one body: the unions never did. They presented separate demands, came up for conflict separately and were separately beaten. This was true, to a greater or less degree, in all trades.

Where the workers held obstinately to the craft form of organization (as in the American steel trade, for example) their unions were often extinguished. Elsewhere they were compelled to make changes, and these changes were always in the direction of enlarging the union to include all workers within one industry. (Some propagandists advocated " one big union " for all workers; this propaganda only struck root in places like Canada, where the total number of workers is so few that it is possible to handle them in one single body without that being unwieldy.) Mostly, the industrial union was advocated. In a number of cases (as for example the British National Union of Railwaymen) this was realized. Elsewhere, by federation and other methods, the industrial union was merely approximated to.

The syndicalists, or industrial unionists—the two things are the same—saw this process and hastened it. They wished to reorganize all the workers into industrial unions, for more effective conflict with the employers. They would conduct these unions on strictly class-war lines; they would keep no faith with the employers; they would direct a series of strikes which would culminate in the taking over of the various industries by the proper trade unions. Political parties, with their treacheries and manœuvrings, would never have entered in. The revolution would be made outside Parliament.

Yet, though in theory the State was to be " by-passed " in this manner, to ignore it in fact was not so easy. The history of syndicalist action is almost entirely, in fact, a history of violent conflict with State organizations. The conflict was natural and inevitable. The syndicalists, who detested and abused politicians, found those politicians became their natural enemies. Even if the race of politicians had been incapable of bearing malice, still continual conflicts with employers, accompanied by boycott and sabotage, were certain to produce disorders in which the police or soldiers had every temptation to intervene. When, if ever, the syndicalists came near to taking over an industry by force, armed conflict was almost certain.

Also, syndicalist logic was, within its limits, absolutely fearless. Since political action was a dangerous nuisance, and political institutions frauds, then it followed that the disputes and divisions between one state and another were delusions and should be ignored. National sentiments were merely kept alive for purposes of mystification by capitalist education. No man should owe loyalty to Germany, France, Britain or the United States. He should realize that all employers were enemies, and all workers friends. That was the only rule.

Consequently, patriotic institutions must be fought; in particular the " defence forces " of the State in which one lived. The duty of the German worker was to hamstring the German army, and of the French worker to cripple the French army. Direct appeals must be made to the soldiers not to obey any commands to shoot upon their fellow workers. Political agitation for disarmament seemed to syndicalists to be doomed to futility. They had a better way: to paralyse the armies and navies from inside. All syndicalists, before the war, took more or less active part in " Don't shoot " campaigns, which resulted in widespread imprisonments. They did not, however, when the time came, secure in fact any refusals to fight on any large scale.

In this outline we have made no mention of the " general strike myth." The theory of syndicalism, philosophized by M. Sorel, includes an account of a " social general strike " to secure the revolution. This social general strike, the philosopher explained, would never occur in fact, but was " an energizing myth " which would give working men the necessary religious zeal to make the revolution by partial strikes. This is philosophers' nonsense, in a philosopher's study. No myth is " energizing " once it has been labelled as a myth: no fraud is successful when its perpetrator announces it is a fraud. The syndicalists who believed in strike action believed in it as a real thing, and practised it. Their programme is limited but quite clear. As an example we may take the British building trades programme:

> " A. *The form of organization required:* (i) All the workers in one industry in one union. (ii) All the industrial unions in one organization.
>
> " B. (i) Ultimate object: Control of industry in the interest of the community. (ii) Immediate objects: To secure a larger part of the product of Labour by *reduction of hours* and *rise in wages*. This is to be accompanied by an increasing control of industry. . . .
>
> " C. Abolition of sectional strikes and strikes on petty issues. . . . Disappearance of Arbitration Machinery; Disappearance of Contracts; Disappearance of Notices.
>
> " D. . . . A recognition of clashing interests between WORKER AND EMPLOYER."

A theoretical objection to this programme is obvious and was quickly made. If continual strikes, unimpelled by contracts or notices, are carried on with the object of gaining increased wages, shorter hours, and encroaching control, then one of two things must result. Either the campaign is on the whole successful or it is not. If it is on the whole successful the material conditions of the workers improve. In that case their revolutionary temper diminishes. They have no longer " nothing to lose but their chains " and become, like the American workers led by Mr. Gompers, unwilling to jeopardize what they have gained. They are more tempted to work in amity with their employers and interest themselves in tariffs and other devices which appear to benefit both them and the employers. If the campaign is on the whole unsuccessful, the result is no better. Strikes conducted by the revolutionary union are lost, and the probable consequence is known to every union organizer. Union membership falls with a sharp crash. The union is broken up; if there is to hand a moderate, cautious, " respectable " union to take its place the members flock into that.

But whether this theoretical objection be sound or not history never allowed us to discover. The only long-continued experiment in syndicalism passed through such varied experiences that no general line of development can be deduced from it. Particular incidents are highly suggestive, but the whole story is far too highly individual and eccentric for general conclusions to be drawn.

The experiment in question is the Industrial Workers of the World—the I.W.W.—an organization which put greater fear into the hearts of the American employers than anything else has ever done. The effects of this hysterical terror are marked all over American history, and are even written in State Statute books, in the form of " criminal syndicalism " laws which state that anything like the I.W.W. is not allowed to exist.

The I.W.W. was founded in 1905 and still remains, though in a sadly diminished state. Its time of power extends only for seven years—from 1912 to 1919—but they were seven of the most highly coloured years in American history. Based upon the definite declaration that " the working class and the employing class have nothing in common," it swiftly brought a new spirit and technique into industrial battles. Its first great strike, and probably its greatest single success, was at Lawrence (Mass.) in 1912. The methods were not such as small-town employers could stand up to. "*Boycott Lawrence!*" cried their paper. "*Railroad men: Lose their cars for them! Telegraphers: Lose their messages for them! Expressmen: Lose their packages for them! Boycott Lawrence! Boycott to the limit!* Let nothing, cars, messages, packages, mails or anything whatsoever that bears the sign, label or address of an official of the Wool Trust, or of a bank, business house or prostituted newspaper which favours them, or of a judge, policeman or cossack or anyone who lends the slightest aid to the millowners go on its way undisturbed."

More direct aids to the solidarity of the strike were taken over from traditional American trade union methods. Paul Brissenden, the sympathetic historian of the I.W.W., quotes the following without disclaiming it:

" The addresses of the men working are given to a committee. They are visited after nine o'clock at night by strangers, generally Poles: ' Working to-day ? ' ' Yah.' (The man speaking has a sharp knife and is whittling a stick.) ' Work to-morrow ? ' ' I d'no.' ' If you work to-morrow, I cut your throat.' ' No, no: I no work.' ' Shake.' And they shake hands."

Personal violence and " cutting throats," however, were no real part of I.W.W. tactics. The I.W.W. theory was that all property was stolen and consequently no respect should be shown to it in industrial conflicts. Destruction and sabotage were permissible and even necessary. But killing was another matter. There was a war on, and if blackleg workers deliberately put themselves in the firing-line they might, unfortunately, get hurt. But " bumping off " as a method of advancing the Social Revolution was an anarchist, not a " wobbly," idea.

From the Lawrence strike onwards the I.W.W. was involved in a bitter and unceasing war, from state to state and from town to town, with not only business men but government authority. Their declaration of war was answered by a similar declaration from the other side, and the chambers of commerce easily outdid the " Reds " in savagery. " Free speech fights "—fights merely to be allowed to speak and to exist—before long bulked larger in I.W.W. history than regular strikes. Special laws outlawing them were in time enacted in half the states of the Union.

Yet, for all the turmoil it created, the I.W.W. was essentially a small organization. Economic and social histories of the States would suggest that it was a gigantic conspiracy. It had an enormous constitution on paper. According to its first plan, named from its author " Father O'Hagerty's Wheel," it had hundreds of sub-organizations. But it is highly doubtful whether more than 300,000 members at most ever passed through its organization. I mean,

that all who ever held " red cards " at any time cannot have amounted to more than that. It is pretty
certain that, after the great block of the Western
Federation of Miners had fallen away, its membership
never reached 100,000 at any one time. Its average
probably varied between 10,000 and 20,000.

But these ten to twenty thousand possessed—were
required indeed by circumstances to possess—
qualities that made them far more dangerous to the
established order than a hundred times their number
of conventional socialists and trade unionists. To
face the conflict that they had provoked, and that
their foes carried to lengths they had never anticipated, all " wobblies " had to have courage and
determination sufficient to pass through continual
violence and affront the possibility of a peculiarly
brutal death. To do this was only possible for men
who had substituted affection for their class for all the
usual paraphernalia of patriotism and religion. A
passionate loyalty to their fellows and a hatred of the
capitalist—a burning love-and-hate—carried them
through unheard-of ordeals with a calmness which
onlookers thought either superhuman or bestial.

Nor were those ordeals " unheard-of " only in a
journalistic sense. Punishments were devised or
revived for them which the world had truly not
heard of for a long time.

As late as 1919 the American Legion, parading in
Centralia, Washington, on Armistice Day, decided to
storm the I.W.W. Hall and sack it, as they had done
before. They entered firing. The I.W.W., true to its

theory of class warfare, tried no pacifist tactics: it fired back. There was of course no earthly chance for the wobblies. The hall was gutted and most of its defenders captured. Wesley Everest, ex-soldier, escaped through the back door, pursued by the mob. He kept them off awhile with his revolver, but was captured in a vain effort to ford the river. They kicked him and beat his front teeth in with a rifle-butt. They put a rope round his neck. "You haven't got the guts to lynch a man in the daylight," he said.

He knew them too well. They put him in a prison cell, maimed and bleeding. Late that night they came back for him. First the whole lights of the centre of the town were extinguished from the power-station. Then the centre door of the jail was broken in and the lynchers came in unresisted. Everest stood up. "Tell the boys I died for my class," was all he said. They beat him down again so that he was helpless and had to be dragged to the waiting motors. The rich and powerful cars drove off, and as they did so all the lights came on again. Inside one of the cars was Everest—half-conscious, one hopes, for the men inside were slicing off his genitals with a razor. He was not dead by the time they reached Chehalis River bridge. A rope was tied to a bridge girder and to his neck, but he could not jump; he had to be kicked over the edge. One of his hands gripped the edge of the bridge. A business man stamped on his fingers till he let go. He hung. Then they pulled up the rope, to find he was not quite dead. He was flung over, with a longer rope, this time to die. He was lifted a second time, found to be dead and swung off again. The head-lights of a great car was turned on to him and in its glare the lynchers fired volleys into his body till they were satisfied. Later the rope was cut and what was left of the body slid into the river.

Such hideous events were repeated again and again. Before this, Frank Little had been murdered in Butte, Montana, dragged alive in the road behind a car. Mob violence was reinforced by legal frame-ups: the possession of a " red ticket " was an almost certain passport to conviction in many places, even before the " criminal syndicalism laws " were passed. But the extraordinary powers of resistance of the I.W.W. stood up to it all. For them nothing seemed to matter but the cause and the sufferings of their martyrs to be welcomed as so much the more effective propaganda. At the great trial in Sacramento the defendants, declaring the court prejudiced and an enemy court, refused to speak. They sacrificed what chances of lighter sentences they might have had for the splendid propaganda of that great silent defence.

Later, in Leavenworth prison, sentenced to ten years, they and others refused, in the less wild times of 1922, to apply to the President for pardon. " We are told that we must either beg mercy for a crime that we did not commit," they wrote to him, " or remain in prison. We do not feel disposed to lie ourselves into freedom." The closing words of their letter might have surprised those who thought that they were only a gang of brutal and illiterate thugs:

> " There are at present only a hundred-odd men in Leavenworth who were here when we arrived. Even the confessed and convicted German spy receives commutation without application, while we are expected to beg for mercy.
>
> " Seven of our number have died, four have gone insane, two with virulent tuberculosis are slowly dying in the steel-barred T.B. ward. One boy is doing his third year in isolation, in the Hole. There is not one of us who will not bear the scars of the prison until he dies.
>
> " We rest our case, Mr. President, with the highest court of all, the great mass of thinking workers of America. We know that if they could know the truth about our case, they would not consent to our further imprisonment.
>
> " To those who do know the truth, we say: ' *Go, traveller, to Sparta and say that we lie here on the spot at which we were stationed to defend our country.*' "

The influence of the I.W.W. spread far beyond its ranks. Its exploits became a saga, and its songs were on the lips of half the workers of America. Stealing a tactic from the Salvation Army, it seized every popular tune and fitted class-war words to them— words that have often outlived the ephemeral originals. What were the first words of " Casey Jones " few people know: the song for ever now is:

> *The workers said to Casey " Won't you help us win this strike ? "*
> *But Casey said " Let me alone; you'd better take a hike,"*

F

*Then someone put a bunch of railroad ties across the track,*
*And Casey hit the river with an awful crack.*

*Casey Jones hit the river bottom,*
*Casey Jones broke his blooming spine,*
*Casey Jones became an Angeleno,*
*He took a trip to heaven on the S.P. line.*

" Steamboat Bill " became " Scissor Bill," the non-union man.

*Scissor Bill, he is a little dippy*
*Scissor Bill, he has a funny face.*
*Scissor Bill should drown in Mississippi*
*He is the missing link that Darwin tried to trace.*

The " Sweet Bye and Bye ":

*Long-haired preachers come out every night,*
*Try to tell you what's wrong and what's right;*
*But when asked how 'bout something to eat*
*They will answer with voices so sweet:*
  *You will eat, bye and bye,*
  *In that glorious land above the sky;*
  *Work and pray, live on hay,*
  *You'll get pie in the sky when you die.*

The story of the I.W.W. has never been fully written. It remains in the minds and the mouths of men of the time, and as time goes on becomes more embellished and more uncertain. The writer of most of the best wobbly songs, Joe Hill, was killed in Utah. His death was, according to the I.W.W., a frame-up. His last words were: " Don't mourn for me, boys, organize." His case is one of the most famous of the

I.W.W. cases. But the story is different in the mouth of each teller.

But this saga came to an end. All this energy and enthusiasm ran into the sand: no Babbitt now ever trembles at the name of the I.W.W. External causes partly are responsible. The ferocity of the repression, increasing from the moment that America went into the war, continued so long that even the strongest spirit might be broken. The source of recruits was tampered with and half-stopped when the Communist International laid a ban on all revolutionary organizations not of an orthodox character and organization. The great prestige of the Russian Revolution was behind that decision, and the younger rebels were drawn away from the I.W.W. But economic causes were probably the final disease. The fighting units of the I.W.W., in its heyday, were drawn from trades which were migratory, or at least unsettled—hoboes, timber-workers, longshoremen, dockers, miners. They took the name of " bums " as a proud label. The essence of their strength lay in the fact of their freedom from ties. Their army was an army of people literally with nothing to lose. It could be, and was, concentrated suddenly on any given place where there was a free speech or other fight on—and if there was no such fight it would start one. But with the change in American conditions that type of labour has become less typical and less important. It might be said that with the end of the " colonizing " period of America, and the occupying of the last piece of free land, the end of the I.W.W.'s epic period was decided. There was a gradually lessening demand for this type of migrant labour.

Its place has been taken by another army, the army of unemployed. But this army, though it is often swayed by the same emotions as were the wobblies, is no possible material for industrial unionist organization. It cannot strike: out-of-works have nothing to strike against. It cannot be organized into industrial unions, for its members have no industries to belong to. The great fighting organization of the industrial unionists has passed away, and there seems no likelihood, in any part of the world, of another such organization appearing.

# CHAPTER IV

## ANARCHISM

" Murder is the killing of a human being, and I
have never heard that a policeman is a human
being."

" At the critical moment the executioner's block
must ever be before the eyes of the revolutionist.
Either he is cutting off the heads of his enemies or his
own is being cut off. Science gives us means which
make it possible to accomplish the wholesale destruction of these beasts quietly and deliberately."

" Those of the reptile brood (capitalists) who are
not put to the sword remain as a thorn in the flesh of
the new society; hence it would be both foolish and
criminal not to annihilate utterly this race of
parasites."

THESE attractive observations are not taken out of a
play, nor are they invented by Press reporters. They
are well-authenticated and considered utterances of
the great American anarchist, Johann Most, and they
were taken as a guide by a very considerable number
of people last century. Nor have we any right, in
considering methods of social change, to refuse the
ear to Johann Most. He only expressed the common
sense of Caiaphas. If a little economical extirpation
of prominent capitalists would put an end to the

present system, which of us dare say that he prefers the continuance of slums, starvation and war to the lives of a few business men ?

Extirpation of individuals is a very grim and disgusting business. It may—indeed, it does—not only terrify the people threatened but degrade and brutalize the people who use it. Nevertheless, for the purpose of this study, it is necessary to inquire not whether it revolts us in itself but whether it is a possible method of revolution. Both assassins and victims may be dragged down by it to a savage level; but if at the end it could be proved, as many very earnest and honourable thinkers have believed, that a new and nobler society would result, then we have no right to refrain from considering it.

It is perfectly true that Anarchism (which is strong in Spain alone to-day) does not consist only of propaganda of individual assassination. The theory of anarchism is far more than that. It is, indeed— in certain aspects a theory of excessive gentleness, a theory that thinks too well, not too ill, of human nature. If we remember Kropotkin, and not Most or Bakunin, we remember arguments to the effect that all coercion is unnecessary and evil, and a sketch of an ideal society of free, federal communism, in which there is no State and no ordering about; but, just because the poison of property and its attendant greeds have been removed, men live in kindliness and simple peace. Every decent man, we feel then, is an anarchist: for surely the object of all these struggles for social reform or revolution is just that—to secure complete freedom, and to remove from life that element of savage struggle for the right to live which is at the root of the hatreds, miseries and greeds of to-day. There is not a man of sensibility who supports restrictions on personal liberty without a sigh, and without hoping for the day when universal education, good feeding, and proper housing will eliminate from our midst the causes of the distorted minds and wounded bodies that make restrictions necessary. The most rigid State socialists and authoritarians have had to admit the truth of the Anarchists' central thesis: Lenin, no friend to Anarchy, wrote what is probably his most important book (*The State and Revolution*) largely to show how it might be reconciled with the Marxist programme.

The chief difference, indeed, between Anarchism and Marxism on the purely theoretical side is merely that Anarchism antedates a process that Marxist Socialism also anticipates, but puts in the distant future. Anarchism claims that as a result of the revolution the State must promptly disappear. Marxism strikes out the word " promptly." Marxism claims that the proletariat, needing a fighting organization to make the revolution, will continue to need it after the revolution until such time as all traces of capitalist organization are removed. Till then, the proletariat must defend itself against a possible come-back by its opponents. It will need a coercive organization, and the organ of coercion, as both disputants agree, is the State. When a classless Communist society is established, no such coercion will be needed and the State will automatically " wither away."

But this " withering away " is dated for the distant future. Proposals that the Russian State should now, seventeen years after the revolution, begin to wither away are officially and vehemently discouraged. Indeed, the whole theory is a distant hypothesis. Once the mental diseases and oppressions that result from poverty and class struggles are forgotten things, it is certainly conceivable that most of the reasons for coercion will have vanished. But even then it is a hardy man who will say that *no* occasion for coercion will remain. There are likely, so long as men and women remain, to be possibilities of quarrel and efforts at oppression. Not all violence arises from economic causes: there is also, for example, sex.

But we need not consider this at length. We are not discussing the ideal State, but methods of reaching it. And to investigate the Anarchist method we must turn from Kropotkin to Bakunin and Most. This method is double, and it contains the largest possible element of coercion. The two parts are: the method of " Propaganda by Deed," and the method of disciplined organization. These are the only two contributions to revolutionary methods offered by Anarchism which are of the least value to us to-day.

" Propaganda by deed " includes theft and forging of money, but its most effective and sensational form is individual assassination. The justification for theft and forgery is simple. Whatever property exists is the proceeds of robbery. The workers have been robbed: to take back some of their losses in order to aid them to recover the whole is not only a permissible act, it is a laudable and necessary act. As for forging money—what imbecility to respect the claim of the State, the chief enemy of the workers, to have the sole right to issue money! The justification for individual murder is not much more difficult. Every day workers are killed by machinery, by pit accidents, by industrial diseases, by unemployment, by foul housing, by starvation. They are killed in these ways because certain other people must make profits. Those people are directly responsible for these deaths. It is mere cant, the Anarchist declares, to say that employers are " caught up in the system " and " cannot help themselves." They, both employers and shareholders, are able to help themselves and are individually guilty. They are not forced to take profits. Perhaps an employer who deliberately and genuinely limited his takings to the wages of his lowest-paid employee might escape his individual guilt. But there are no such employers or shareholders. They all take all the profits they can: however " advanced " they may be in theory they recoil in horror when it is proposed that their dividends, their personal unearned income, should be taken away from them. " Not that! Not that! " they cry as loudly and with a far more genuine horror than the heroines of melodrama.

These people who by their own will and their own greed are guilty of murder, have signed their death warrant. They can only be stopped by an execution.

There is but one argument that will overmaster their fear of losing their income, the argument of a greater fear. The Anarchist sees himself as the judge and hangman for the workers. He says to selected victims, to notorious enemies and oppressors of the workers: " For your crimes you shall die. If you call on your hired gangsters, whom you name statesmen and policemen, to shoot and kill for you, they shall die, too. And your fate will terrify your fellows and break down their resistance to the revolution."

Such a threat as this is almost as frightening as the threat the I.W.W. made to American society. Moreover it needs fewer people to sustain it. The I.W.W. was a body of picked men, it is true, but after all it ran into tens of thousands. The blows it hit were heavy thumping blows, the blows of mass action. The blow of the Anarchist is a solitary sharp steel stab, the thin piercing of a stiletto to the heart. It must not, as a method, be dismissed as ineffectual.

It has been tested out only once on a satisfactorily extensive scale. This was in France in 1891 and 1892. The conflict began on May 1st of the former year. At Levallois-Perret in Paris, the Anarchists were holding a demonstration, with red and black banners. The police fell upon them, beating them and endeavouring to seize their banners—a purely instinctive action on the part of French policemen. The Anarchists replied with revolvers. The police fired back. There was a considerable battle, six policemen and three Anarchists being injured. Eventually the police were victorious. Among their prisoners was a severely injured man called Decamps, who was brought to trial in August. The trial was even more prejudiced than usual. The judge actually refused Decamps permission to speak and " railroaded " him to prison forthwith.

Early next year the Anarchists began their counter-attack. Dynamite was secured by a robbery of a factory on February 14th. Less than a month later the first bomb exploded: Benoit, the judge who had sentenced Decamps, found his house on the Boulevard St. Germain half destroyed. Four days later the Lobau barracks, the centre of Paris's armed forces, was bombed. Twelve days later the house of Bulot, Minister of Justice when Decamps was condemned, was bombed, the first floor being blown out.

The police were scurrying like rabbits about Paris by now. At last an informer was found: it was a waiter named L'herot, who worked in a restaurant where certain Anarchists used to meet. The police descended on the man he indicated. The man was named Ravachol: he promptly admitted—indeed, claimed would be a juster word—two out of three of the bombings. Before he could be brought to trial a bomb was exploded in the restaurant where the waiter worked. The waiter escaped, but the proprietor was killed and a customer badly injured.

The Anarchists won the first round. Ravachol was brought to trial and a trembling jury acquitted him.

Not for long, however. In a few months' time he was rearrested, condemned and executed. He had killed a miser called " the hermit of Chambles " and seized his hoard for the Cause. It was also proved that he had robbed tombs of jewellery, put false money into circulation, and dynamited property.

Ravachol dead, the battle had only just begun. The Chamber of Deputies met shortly after the tragedy. The galleries had the usual crowd of spectators. A man arose in a front seat, his arm stretched above his head, holding a small black object in his hand. Before the bomb could be thrown a woman struck his arm: the black egg flew wide and struck the chandelier. There was a frightful explosion, a sharp scream, smoke, and the shouting of frightened politicians. The President of the Chamber, alone keeping his head, called out " The session will continue."

When the assassin was arrested he gave his name as Auguste Vaillant. He regretted that only one deputy and a few spectators had been hurt. " As in this duel," he said, " I have only wounded my adversary, it is now his turn to strike me." Members of the house of deputies, headed by the wounded deputy, appealed to President Carnot not to carry out the death sentence. It had long been the custom in France not to behead for a murder which was only a murder in intention. But the President refused: Vaillant was guillotined.

Just a few days after his death some guests were arriving for dinner at the Hotel Terminus. They were listening to the music: the scene was one of typical upper-middle-class elegance. Suddenly through the window was hurled the terrible oval black missile—a loud explosion followed and the floor and tables were covered with wounded and fainting. Outside, two or three quick-witted policemen were fighting savagely with a tall, dark, sullen-looking man, the bomb-thrower. His name was Emile Henry.

The case of Henry did more than any other to increase the terror which was freezing the hearts of the French bourgeoisie. Henry turned out to be a man utterly unknown to the police. He was silent, solitary and morose: he had never been connected with any disturbance. No policeman could ever have suspected him. Nor could his victims have anticipated their fate. Henry had no grievance against them. They were a gathering of exploiters about to indulge themselves in feasting at the expense of the workers. They were no more guilty and also no more innocent than any others: therefore, Henry had bombed them. " In this pitiless war which we have declared on the bourgeoisie," he told the court, " we ask no pity. We give death and know how to suffer it. That is why I await your verdict with indifference." It seemed to the French bourgeois that each one of them, individually, sitting harmless at his dinner was liable to a sudden and hideous death, even if he had no quarrel to his knowledge with any man; and that not the cleverest detective could anticipate from where the blow could come. To exacerbate this fear, Henry threw in the information that he had been responsible for several other explosions which had baffled the police during the last year or two. One had been a counter-attack on the Carnaux Mining Company for breaking a miners' strike. He had planted a bomb in the company's office: before it could kill the manager it had been removed by the police. But at least it blew up the police station, putting an end to the station sergeant and three policemen.

President Carnot again resisted all appeals for mercy, and Henry, though no Terminus guest had died, was executed. The President was not unconscious of the terror around him, but considered a firm front and courage were alone needed to defeat the threat. He went down to Lyons to open the Great Exposition with more than usual ostentation.

He walked, that light June evening, a distinguished bearded figure in black, *portefeuille* beneath his arm, eminent top-hatted friends with him, towards the entrance to a theatre. The head of the Republic was not afraid of a few Anarchists. As he stood chatting, a dark figure leapt from the crowd upon him. With scarcely a groan he fell down: his assailant was seized at once by furious hands. He did not resist: he stood looking at what lay before him. The President was dead: in his heart was a knife on whose handle was engraved the word " Vaillant."

The murderer, an Anarchist named Caserio, was arrested and with his crowning exploit the Anarchist campaign concluded. No other equally formidable campaign of " propaganda by deed " has ever been conducted by the Anarchists, nor is any more perfect specimen likely to be produced in the future.

Yet what results were achieved by all this sacrifice and cunningly directed violence ? Practically none. The political constitution of the French Republic was scarcely shaken, let alone the economic oppression of the workers. At the end of this terrifying series of attacks the position of the workers was worse rather than better. The governing class had not surrendered. How could it surrender ? To surrender, one must have an opposing force, capable of occupying the country, to whom to surrender. There was no such force. Neither President Carnot nor his successor, however great their fear, could have thrown up the sponge. They could not even have found the desperate men, solitary and numbering only one in a hundred thousand, who were directing these attacks. They had to fight, and their fear made them fight more savagely. The results showed that, under such a threat, a capitalist state could always crush the Anarchists. The *lois scelerates* which were passed and applied with almost complete disregard for individual liberty ended in the expulsion or imprisonment of practically every Anarchist. All Socialist and Liberal activities were stopped and every bolt-hole and hiding-place inspected until every Anarchist or possible Anarchist was under bars or out of France. The working class was deprived of its most necessary defences while this went on; and its own disapproval of the Anarchists' policy made it even more difficult for it to resist.

It is reasonable to deduce from this that a highly skilled system of private assassination is a very feeble weapon in the struggle for social advancement: indeed it is probably a positive hindrance. But a development of the Anarchist argument is current to-day in circles which have suffered from Fascism, especially among German and Italian refugees. They argue that Fascism is a new development of capitalism which was unknown to Most and the classical Anarchists. Under Fascism, they argue, a single leader (or at the most half a dozen leaders) concentrates in his person all the coercive power of capitalism. Because the difficulties of capitalism have forced the capitalist class to put all its authority into the hands of one dictator, therefore, it is suggested, it is now true that the assassination of Hitler, Mussolini, or Starhemberg would shatter that authority and leave the way open to a swift and relatively painless change.

This argument is often reinforced by an emotional appeal. The crimes which are ascribed, apparently with ample evidence, to these individuals are recounted and we are asked whether we wish to plead for the lives of such monsters. But this is an appeal we ought not consider; at least, not in this book. We are not constituting ourselves public executioners on moral grounds; we are considering whether certain forms of action will or will not lead to a social revolution.

The moment we look at the problem from this angle we see that such a policy is still futile.

Whatever be the personal abilities of eminent men, whether they be leaders of the bourgeoisie or misleaders of the workers, these abilities are never irreplaceable. Presidents, kings, dictators, financiers and captains of industry are articles which are infinitely replaceable from the same stocks. It is the social system which produces them regularly and certainly which must be put out of action. To slay them is like scratching spots to cure chicken-pox.

Yet, if individual assassination is rejected perhaps the other distinctive Anarchist method may be worth investigating. In speaking of this method it must be remembered that Anarchists are two very different kinds of people. "Philosophical Anarchists" tend to be mild and rather tedious persons, often of a certain amount of worldly wealth, who live in communities, preach rather than practise free love, and write essays upon the advantages of perfect freedom from law. Their communities are incapable of growth, and for that reason are harmless; they are sometimes vexed by police officers, but only because they offend some respectable neighbour's inhibitions or because they have become entangled with unphilosophical Anarchists; they are far less common to-day than they were thirty or fifty years ago. Contrasted with them are the active Anarchists, who, holding the same theories about the aim of the revolution and the viciousness of delegated authority, nevertheless see that rigorous discipline is necessary to make a change. They consider that armed insurrection, combined with violent strike action, is the only method which carries sufficient power behind it to break the resistance of the ruling class. But to direct such a

G

movement picked men acting together are necessary. Large democratic bodies—which the Anarchist in principle suspects—could never do this. They must be controlled by a selected body of men responsible to their own consciences alone, but organized in a secret and immensely powerful organization. These men will enter into larger organizations—trade unions, co-operatives, or what you will—and see that they are brought into line and used in the struggle. If these bodies are smashed thereby, so much the worse for them. The intelligent Anarchist goes on to control the next organization that is thrown up. He may be a rigid Anarchist, who will allow no central control over his local group. If so, his influence is small and local. If he is not, if he follows the teaching of Bakunin and Nechayeff, he admits that central, disciplined control of an international society is, for this one purpose alone, necessary. With that decision, he becomes a person of importance, and his theories become a possibly effective means of social change.[1]

These tactics were effectively applied by Bakunin in the First International against Marx, in the years 1869 to 1872. His general headquarters were situated in Switzerland, and the organizations he had under

[1] I have already stated that these views are typical of only one-half of the Anarchists. Perhaps I should repeat this. Miss Emma Goldman, for example, at a lecture given by myself in 1933 vehemently repudiated them, with a squat anger that was at her age truly remarkable. " These views," she said, " are not true Anarchism. They are the product of the Anarchism of the Latin races, and should not be considered by us."

his hand were too secret, too deliberately confusing for us to give a full account of them. The objects of the bodies which he headed were double—(i) to compel the International to abandon ordinary political action and to take up insurrectionary organization instead, (ii) to break up the General Council, which Marx dominated, and replace it by autonomous national organizations, which the Anarchists would more easily control. Bakunin had to his hand a most complex and puzzling network of secret societies, complete with passwords and cryptic alphabets. Tentatively, we may say that it appears probable that the organization was like a Chinese doll, one figure within the other. The outer organization was the International, the great working-class body he was seeking to dominate. Within this was his own avowed organization, called the Alliance of Social Democracy. This, the penetrating body, was without its knowledge controlled by an organization of National Brothers, of whom nothing much is known. Controlling these again were—if they ever really existed, for sometimes one doubts whether these are not dream-organizations—one hundred International Brothers, the Cardinals of the Revolution. There was also, about 1872, a further organization called simply " Y," and concerning that there is no reliable information whatever.

At the end of a long and vexatious inquiry the only definite statement that can be made is that while Bakunin was at the height of his power the European Labour movement was honeycombed with secret societies, some of which were no doubt very silly, melodramatic and ineffective, but some of which were determined and dangerous bodies. In the upshot, Bakunin found that he had taken on, in Marx and Engels, adversaries as tough as himself. He was driven out of the International, but in being expelled he tore it in pieces, and it was seventeen years before it could be re-formed.

In his campaign to control it he used distortion of the truth, ballot-stuffing, fake mandates, and deception extensively. He did this on principle, and with a zeal that can only come from a really altruistic impulse. He wanted, as he told his Lyons lieutenant, Richard, the triumph " not of my person, not of *a* power, but of *our* power, the power of our collectivity in whose favour I am ready to abdicate my name and personality." He had studied, he told the same follower, the organization of the Jesuits, and proposed to adopt their methods whole-heartedly.

Nechayeff, his more whole-hearted follower, agreed with him, and, doubting of the single-mindedness of his leader, turned his own methods against him. Bakunin, in his surprise and annoyance, has recorded these methods in full and fairly dramatically. They are methods which continually attract serious but hasty revolutionaries, especially immature pseudo-Communists. I have myself heard them frequently advocated, and even inexpertly practised, by men who would have shuddered at the thought that they were anything but " disciplined young Leninists, free of Leftward deviations."

" All this," wrote Bakunin, speaking of Nechayeff's aspirations, " is very natural, legitimate and exceedingly useful, but the way in which he goes about it is detestable. Under the impression of the catastrophe which has just ruined the Russian secret organization, he has slowly convinced himself that to erect a serious indestructible association one must take as basis Machiavelli's politics and adopt fully the system of the Jesuits—for body nothing but violence, for soul a lie.

" Truth, mutual confidence and serious and severe solidarity only exist among a dozen people who are the *sanctum sanctorum* of the society. All the rest are to serve as blind tools, as material for exploitation by these dozen really united men. You are permitted, indeed you are ordered, to deceive them, compromise them, rob them and at need to ruin them. They are conspiracy-fodder. . . . The sympathy of mild men, who are only partly devoted to the revolution and who besides it have other human interests like love, friendship, family, social relationships—such sympathy is not in his eyes a sufficient foundation, and in the name of the cause he must gain possession of all your person, without your knowledge. To do this, he will spy on you and get to know all your secrets; if he is alone in your rooms he will open all your drawers, read all your letters, and when a letter appears interesting—which means compromising in any way for you or a friend—he will steal it and keep it carefully as evidence against you or your friend."

Bakunin cited examples of this, of Nechayeff's

skilfully breaking up too dangerous or powerful friendships by spreading slander and inventing intrigues, of his endeavouring to seduce young women and land them with babies " to increase their revolutionary protest," and reports Nechayeff's own deliberate defence of his policy, before a committee set up to judge him. " Well, yes, that is so," he said. " It is our system. We consider as enemies, and it is our duty to deceive and compromise, all persons who are not *completely* with us." He explained that this category included all who were not convinced of the correctness of this method and had not promised to apply it themselves.

These methods have a certain attraction: nevertheless it appears that they should be rejected. They should be rejected, that is to say, as ineffective—not on moral grounds. This book is, so far as the writer can make it, a strictly objective study, and therefore we are not entitled to refuse to consider any method to attain a better state of society because it offends our moral prejudices. The world has always admired the Roman who sacrificed his son to save the republic: we cannot refuse to cut the throats of Labour Parties and Co-operatives, and to lie to our best friends, if it seems necessary to the same end. We can only reject measures which appear ineffectual, not measures which we think repulsive. We shall be dead a long time, and our corpses will stink, anyway. Our æsthetic scruples will appear unsavoury too if they are responsible for the continuance of misery and oppression on earth.

Two main objections, then, to Anarchist methods appear to be valid. The first is that the whole policy is based on an assumption of the loyalty and integrity of the Anarchists themselves. This is a wild assumption. Anarchist bodies, by their very structure, are the happy homes of police spies. The *provocateur* and strong-arm man asks nothing better than an organization whose *entrée* is secured by violent language and a skill in the use of passwords, crook methods, black masks and private murder. The Anarchist organization, itself so skilfully pulling the wires of a larger body, dances on wires that lead straight back to the Prefecture of Police. In Catalonia, for example, the time-honoured capital of Anarchy, the Anarchist bombs have regularly been fired off at exactly the moments most suitable to the Spanish Conservative Party, as is shown in Mr. McCabe's *Spain in Revolt*. No proof can be brought in such matters, but short of direct proof the evidence of time and occasion points directly to the greatest Anarchist force in the world having been regularly the deluded instrument of clerical reaction.

A further false assumption is the gullibility of the members of trade unions, peace societies, co-operative guilds, and so forth. The cynic tends to believe that elderly trade union officials and middle-class " progressive persons " are almost unplumbably silly and deceit-worthy: he asks himself if there is any idiocy the one will not be guilty of, or any story of oppression the other will not believe. But this is a cynic's belief. There is a point at which even these people will observe that they are being used as cannon-fodder; and behind them is a large mass of persons, largely working class, who are not so easily deceived by phrases. When they are thrown to the dogs in a hopeless strike " to promote revolutionary feeling," the suffering is felt in their own homes. They are intimately made aware of what this " intensification of class war " means, and vent their feelings upon the amateur Grand General Staff which has led them into it.

The aphorism of Trotsky, one of the greatest living strategists of class struggle, is worth bearing in mind: " It is permissible," he wrote, " to lie to and deceive the enemies of the working class as extensively as you can. It is never permissible, in any circumstances, to lie to or deceive the working class itself." Such an action is counter-revolutionary, however worthy the intentions of the liar may be. He is trapping and confusing his own forces instead of the enemy's. Your troops, to use a military metaphor, must know for whom and why they are fighting, or they will quickly abandon the battle. If you treat them as sheep, they will behave as sheep, and sheep are always defeated.

There are few instances in history of the Anarchist method being tested. By far the best is the history of Spain in 1873. The severed portion of the International in Spain was entirely under Bakunin's influence. It was a large and powerful organization, containing 23,000 determined men—a formidable force in Spain of that day. The constitution of Spain at that moment gave it its opportunity. The President of the Republic was the high-minded but ineffectual Pi y Margall, the chief of the "benevolos" or Platonic Republicans. He was opposed by the Unitary Republicans and the Intransigeants. The Anarchists of Alcoy in Alicante took advantage of his high principles to seize the town. Pi y Margall, rather than coerce them, resigned. His place was taken by another Republican, Salmeron, who behaved in a most un-Platonic manner. He sent troops. The Anarchists of Alcoy thereupon patched up an arrangement with the local bourgeoisie by which the municipal power was shared between the two. After this, as a result of the infinite complexities of Spanish politics, the Intransigeants rose in revolt. The Anarchists joined in, and in certain places—for example, San Lucar de Barrameda—were able so to direct the masses as to take control. But they went down to ruin. The Intransigeants were defeated and with them fell the Anarchists. They had no firm grip upon the masses, and were further hampered by a belief that after their victory the State must disappear. They had therefore no idea of organizing a powerful revolutionary State, nor had they any understanding and reliable defenders of it if they had. They were able to ride the whirlwind when it rose, but when it fell they dropped to the ground with a lamentable thump. In 1874 Emilio Castelar and General Pavia carried out a *coup d'état* against the Cortes. In the course of it they almost casually put an end to the legal existence and political power of the International in Spain. That was the end.

# CHAPTER V

BLANQUISM

To clutter up a study like this with the theories of unknown or forgotten prophets of social change would be to be a pedantic nuisance. The showing off of scholarly knowledge is at all times regarded as vulgar proceeding—though why, when it is permissible to exhibit fine clothes or physical excellence, goodness only knows. Perhaps it is because the possession of an unusual and painfully acquired knowledge of obscure theorists arouses the collector's spirit, and its possessor becomes as odious an exhibitionist bore as a stamp collector or a Don Juan. Or it may be that certain faculties at certain universities are overstaffed and underworked and have to make work for themselves; or it may be that the writers of Ph.D. theses are really inspired by a retroactive form of Messiah-hunting, which makes them seek in some dead second-rater the inspiration which their contemporaries find in living technocrats and currency reformers. But whatever be the reason, the disease is a real and repulsive one; and for that reason the present writer has some diffidence in bringing before the reader's notice the name of Louis Auguste Blanqui.

But though Blanqui is forgotten in England and

America, he is not forgotten in the country of his origin, and he was for years a European figure of great importance. Of course, his name is not to be found in ordinary text-books. But in studying revolutionary history we are studying a history which is entirely independent of orthodox history, though it runs parallel to it. The two histories are both quite accurate, but they are about two different sets of people, the governing class and the governed. Sometimes, in Paris in 1871, or in Russia in 1917, the history of the lower class thrusts its unwelcome snout up into the history of the upper so vigorously that it cannot be ignored; but otherwise official history may be very satisfactorily written (and often is) by men as ignorant of the working class and the farmers as if they were detective-story writers. Therefore, that text-books carry no mention of Blanqui means very little. The Blanquist party has the same claim to our notice that the Anarchists and the "wobblies" have—that it made several serious attempts to change society and some appeared to be nearly successful.

Indeed, the Blanquists controlled the Paris Commune of 1871, the body which for nearly fifty years was the sole instance in history of a working-class State, and to that extent may even claim a superiority over their rivals. Before that they had made several unsuccessful attempts to overturn the French State, and had had a very large part in putting an end to the reign of Napoleon III. After it they remained as an organized party for many years, and the last traces only disappeared during the war. Their ideas survived longer. In 1919, when the newly founded Communist International was attracting to itself all the revolutionary elements across the world, three main currents of opinion could be traced. The first and largest was the traditionally revolutionary Marxist, typified by the Bolsheviks. The second was the Syndicalist, headed by the American I.W.W. The third and last was the Blanquist, represented chiefly by a now extinct German party called the K.A.P.D., which descended directly from the famous Spartakusbund of Karl Liebknecht and Rosa Luxembourg.

Blanquism is very little of a theory; it is a method of action. Blanqui took what theories he had largely from Babeuf. Babeuf, who called himself Gracchus, in 1796 perceived that the French Revolution had left rich rich and poor poor, nor did it show any likelihood of doing anything else. He therefore organized an armed conspiracy, mixed civilians and soldiers, to seize the State and start a Socialist society. He had sense enough to see that eighteenth-century France could not all become Socialist overnight; he therefore drew up a long elaborate plan by which a " community " was organized. This community was to hold all its possessions in common, to direct industrial enterprises in common and cultivate farms co-operatively. It was to have especial privileges over all competitors, and the whole influence of the State would be used to compel, by every form of economic and other pressure short of direct force, the independent employer to join the community. Babeuf's plan was in fact precisely the plan which the Soviet Government eventually applied in the early stages of making Russian agriculture collective. Given a central government as powerful as the Soviet and an army of followers as obstinate and as disciplined as the Russian communists, Babeuf might possibly have been successful. He had at least realized what the supporters of co-operative societies to-day rarely realize—that a co-operative society has only strictly limited powers of expansion within a capitalist régime unless it is given enormous privileges and " unfair " advantages by the State. Schemes which ignore this fact are continually being revived, and perhaps it is necessary to stop to examine the point.

No co-operative movement has ever succeeded in extending its sway beyond certain industries. Certain " co-op " movements have attained enormous size. Since the German and Italian organizations have been extinguished by violence, the English and Scottish movements, headed by the C.W.S. and the S.C.W.S., are probably the premier bodies. Yet even they have found that natural causes have strictly limited their growth. The original hope of co-operators was that the principle of sharing all profits among consumers would spread so widely that ultimately no one would be so foolish as to buy from a private employer. Then the system of private property would have come to a painless, or at least peaceful, end.

These anticipations have never been fulfilled. Co-operation has been able to get a firm foothold in distribution. " T' Co-op shop " in Northern England and Scotland is often the finest store in town. But it has never been able to handle *all* distribution— motor cars, for example, it has signally failed to distribute. Nor has it in any trade, even food and clothing, been able to establish a dominance over private property. When it comes to co-operative production the stop has come even sooner. It produces its own food, soap, textiles and leather, and some furniture. Practically nothing more of importance. Electricity ? Coal ? Shipbuilding ? and the other great trades ? It never has entered into them effectively and to all appearances never will. There is a strange but unfailing automatic stop which closes down co-operative activities at a certain point.

The nature of this stop is fairly easily discerned. The co-ops can handle, and even produce, goods like food and clothes which the working class knows, wants and can judge, and which every working-class wife can criticize. It cannot exploit and handle coal- mines, shipyards and power plants which its demo- cratic controllers know nothing about. Accident may here and there see that a competent man is put in charge—but he is rarely appreciated and is most often bought up by a capitalist rival. It is possible that a workable scheme for controlling a co-operative mine, for example, could be devised : but the con- trollers would have to be the miners, who alone know if the mine is well run, not the working-class housewives in a nearby town, or their nominees, who know nothing at all about it.

Furthermore, in the trades which the " co-ops " can run well they are prevented from extinguishing their rivals by inherent conditions which are all to their credit. There are certain things a co-op *must* not do. It is run by workers who want better living conditions, and it dare not, without outraging its supporters and wrecking its chances of expansion, reproduce the conditions of Messrs. Snatchem and Grab up the road. It has to pay better wages and work shorter hours than its rivals, who, in the distributive trades, usually go to the extremes of sweating that the law will allow. It therefore operates under a steady disadvantage which is equivalent to a tax on sales.

For a co-operative movement to control the whole of distribution, and for it to enter into and control production, it would be necessary for it to be granted exceptional privileges and be quite grossly " favoured " at the expense of its rivals. A government as ruthless as the Bolshevik Government, and as uninhibited, would be needed. And even with that, it is likely that actual confiscation would be needed in cases such as the coal-mines, where natural resources are limited and already in other people's hands.

Blanqui, in taking over Babeuf's plans, was far more interested in his conspiratorial organization than in his community. Discussion of the form of the future State, he said, was in the first place silly, because nobody knew the truth, and in the second dangerous, because it made good revolutionaries fly at each other's throats. Practical steps that a revolutionary government might immediately take interested him, but discussions of the future State, the weakness of the Anarchists, he detested. Paul Lafargue, Marx's precocious pupil, once brought Blanqui an essay on the relative merits of Collectivist and Mutualist societies. " You would have been better employed on a syllabus of primary education," said the grim old man as he dropped it in the waste-paper basket. " Communism and Proudhonism stand by a river bank," was another of his aphorisms, " quarrelling whether the field on the other side is maize or wheat. Let us cross and see."

The instrument of change which he forged was a body of picked armed men. He differed from the Anarchists in two ways. The first, that so far from prophesying the annihilation of the State and so attracting to his standard only those freaks of society who would accept this, his object was enormously to strengthen the State and use it for the achievement of social equality. The second, that though his organization was secret, its secrecy was never directed against the rest of the revolutionary or semi-revolutionary movement, but against the rulers of society. Blanqui never attempted to " white-ant " or honeycomb the trade unions as the Anarchists did the International. His relations with other revolutionary or working-class bodies were confined to public speeches telling them how mistaken they were. His object was to raise a private army against the government. The miseries of the capitalist system would provide the raw material for revolution. Some day the intolerable sufferings of the workers, or some peculiarly outrageous folly or cruelty of their rulers would set the masses moving. Nature would see to that. Then the Blanquists, working among them like goats among sheep, would turn a foaming disorganized demonstration into a cohesive revolutionary army which could not be dispersed by a police charge. Under their direction the strategic points of the city would be seized, instead of energy being dissipated in senseless demonstrations where the police were prepared for them. Overnight the government would find itself in flight. " Forty-eight hours are enough to make a revolution," Blanqui used to say.

Blanqui was the first undemocratic revolutionary: the first man to realize that the granting of the vote to the workers and farmers did not mean that those two classes would necessarily or probably have the skill to organize their own emancipation. He declared that a short period of dictatorship would be needed. He was the first practitioner of that much-feared thing, the " dictatorship of the proletariat." He did not generally use that phrase: he preferred the phrase " revolutionary dictatorship." For two good reasons; the one that the Marxist class-analysis of the revolution which leads to the use of the word " proletariat " was of little interest to him; the other that the phrase itself is misleading. The proletariat

H

itself can never exercise a " dictatorship." It is too large a body. The dictatorship has in fact, in the day-to-day administration, to be exercised " for it " by a small body of chosen persons, Blanquists or Communists.

The organization which he had to construct for this end had obviously to be constructed of selected materials. One of the reasons for the spectacular failures of the Communist parties outside Russia has been that they have too often adopted Blanqui's tactics without Blanqui's recruiting rules. Blanqui had a first and second rank in his followers. The first rank was the army, trusted to go anywhere and do anything. The second was the camp-followers. They might be trusted for certain jobs—speech-making, obstructing the courts and what not—but they could not be trusted with any serious enterprises or with any grave secrets. (Clemenceau was a second-ranker.) Admission to the party, and promotion to the first rank, were not secured by orthodox opinions or freedom from " deviations." The conditions were—ability to keep your mouth shut; personal courage and a knowledge of the use of fire-arms; quickness in directing a crowd and a close natural sympathy with the workers; proved devotion to the revolutionary cause. Added to these should be, as far as possible, a dislike for theoretical arguments and romantic attitudes, which Blanqui considered to be the native vices of French reformers.

Some of the societies that Blanqui organized met with early disaster. One founded in 1838 stays in history largely for its odd names. It was called the *Society of the Seasons*. Each member was a *Day*. *Days* were organized in groups of seven, led by a *Sunday* and called a *Week*. Four *Weeks* made up a *Month*, *Months* were always led by a chief called *July*. Three *Months* made up a *Season*, the *Season's* leader was known as *Spring*. Four *Seasons* made up a *Year*. There were three *Years* in the society. This elaboration did not save the society: it made an ill-chosen attempt at revolution and smashed itself to pieces. Blanqui was sent to prison, where indeed he spent most of his life.

Some twenty years afterwards he was in command of a better-organized force, numbering say two or three thousand. When the news of Sedan came, the anger of the people of Paris was sufficiently great to provide the " raw material " for Blanqui to work upon. He called out the party for September 4th and the fall of the Empire was the result. A first-hand account of the *coup* exists: it is worth quoting as an example of the method of " stiffening " and directing a crowd in actual operation. Balsenq is the name of the writer:

> " The day before September 4th Blanqui gave orders for every Blanquist to go through the Faubourgs to prepare for next day's demonstration, which must at all costs be turned into a revolution. On the morning of the 4th we hunted creatures came out of our dens to place ourselves at the head of our followers, whose rendezvous was fixed at the Place de la Concorde.

" Granger, Edmond Levraud and I arrived there about one. The Place was guarded by soldiers and police, the bridge (leading to the Chamber of Deputies in the Palais Bourbon on the south side) by the Municipal Horseguards, the neighbouring quays by strong detachments of police, and the square of the Palais Bourbon, finally, by troops of the line. The palace itself was guarded by a battalion of National Guards of the 6th *arrondissement*.

" Already the enormous mass of demonstrators had been pushed back into the Champs Élysées, the Cours-la-Reine and the Avenue Gabrielle. The terrace of the Tuileries was black with people. A more active and angry crowd, in which were many students, was massed on the left bank, threatening the Deputies from nearer at hand. . . .

" At this moment a strong thrust was made by the demonstrators. It was the workers from the Faubourgs coming. We recognized friends and placed ourselves at their head. Very quickly we were face to face with the army and National Guard. The moment was tragic. Cries arose, ' Put up your arms! *Vive la République !* ' The opposing forces touched. Energetic and repeated commands were heard from the officers, but the soldiers did not obey. The sea of people pressed forward; the troops, swamped on all sides, gave way.

" A violent surge forward carried us to the head of the bridge, which must be crossed to reach the Palais Bourbon. The police tried in vain to stop the torrent: we gained the bridge and faced the Municipal Guard. There, more anxiety and another surge forward. The guard, packed tighter and

tighter and happily unable to move, let us pass on
the bridge pavements, at the end of which we broke
through three ranks of police and found ourselves in
face of the palace railings, guarded by soldiers. One
commander ordered his men to fix bayonets. A few
obeyed slowly and laughing. I ran up to the officer,
pointed to the mass following us, to convince him
that his orders were useless. Anyway, while I was
talking the railings were passed and I hastily rejoined
the boys. We were in the palace, facing the main
entrance guarded by the National Guard. . . .

" I leapt to the handle to open the double door,
and gripped on to it. The door would not yield, and
the Guards beat me with their rifle-butts till I let go,
exhausted, and returned to my friends, whom the
Guards had prevented from aiding me.

" Fortunately I knew of a door near to the stair of
the tribune and the President's chair. We rushed to
it, Granger, Levraud and myself leading. There, too,
were some National Guards! We thrust them aside.
I put my big shoulders against the door, buttressed
myself with my feet, made a supreme effort which
broke it in and threw me down. In one bound
Granger and Levraud were at the President's chair,
still occupied by Schneider. A student named
Martin who followed us was ringing the President's
bell.

" Granger seized it and cried in a loud voice which
dominated the tumult: ' Citizens, in face of our
disasters and the misfortunes of France, the people of
Paris has invaded this place to proclaim the fall of
the Empire and the Republic. We demand that the
deputies decree this.'

" Silence. The President had bolted. Jules Favre (a Left deputy) climbed to the tribune, pale and anxious. He said: ' Citizens, at the very moment when the people invaded this place, the deputies were deliberating the pronouncement of the fall of the Empire and the proclamation of the Republic. Since the people have penetrated into this Assembly, the Republic should not be proclaimed here, but at the Hotel de Ville.' Though these words may not be exact, I can answer for the general sense.

" Favre left the tribune. The deputies ran— literally. *Sauve qui peut!* The struggle was to get outside first."

So far the Blanquists were victorious. But events that followed immediately showed the weakness inherent in the strength of Blanquism. The great masses had never heard of this group of determined men who had carried them on to success. The group had not sufficient contact with the people to form a government. The government consisted of persons whom the people knew—old-line politicians. The Blanquists had only minor posts, if any. Blanqui became a battalion-commander in the National Guard. Consequently, the Republican government was a lamentable failure from every point of view. The expulsion of Napoleon III seemed hardly worth while.

After the war the history of the Commune showed up another weakness. The Commune was the first working-class government in the world, and should have been the high-water mark of Blanquism, for the

Blanquists were the most numerous party in it. Further, they had had a good share in causing the Thiers Government to run away. Instead of this, the policy of the Commune was wavering and erratic. The Blanquists blundered and perorated. They failed to organize the army properly or extirpate the spies or set on foot any beginning of a Socialist State. This they did simply because Blanqui was absent. Before the Commune had been proclaimed he had been arrested in the provinces. Without him, his followers were sergeants in charge of an army. They had so absorbed military discipline that they could not act without orders. " When *he* comes," was Rigault's favourite phrase: the Communards were waiting for a leader who never came.

It is possible that this is not an inherent fault of Blanquism. If Blanqui had been able to attach to himself men who could take his place—equals, not merely lieutenants—his organization might have justified itself. But still there would have remained the further weakness we have already mentioned. A Blanquist party of its nature has no deep connections with the mass of the workers. It is isolated, and its membership tends to be recruited from intelligent desperate men rather than from trusted members of the working class. It tends to have, as the Anarchists had, an excessive proportion of *déclassés*, and to remain a troop of guerrillas and not an army in the social war. In certain times, when war or unemployment drives large sections of the working class to desperation, they may form an alliance with these *déclassés*, and

organizations like the German " Spartakusbund "
appear.

But of recent years other outlets have been provided for desperate working-class youths. Modern
youths are not trained in French revolutionary
philosophy, and they go where employment and
violence are offered together in one fascinating
proposition. They become Fascists, or Nazis, or
gangsters—if there be any difference between these
three.

# Part III—PRACTICE

## CHAPTER VI

### THE GENERAL STRIKE

WE have now examined all the principal " blue prints " of methods of social change. Let it be explained to those who resent not finding, in these previous chapters, the particular device for credit inflation, or whatever it may be, which they favour, that their medicine has not been omitted through any intent to slight it. We are not considering what measures a government determined to make a social change should apply. We are investigating how the social revolutionaries, mild or ferocious, can become the government. Once there they may apply the theories of Major Douglas, Professor Eisler, Mr. Howard Scott, Joseph Smith, or whomever they please: that is not our affair at the moment.

Since the investigation of theories has not led to any final conclusion as yet—has led us only to reject certain methods, but not to give final approval to any—we must go on to investigate practice. What results, in recorded fact, have been achieved by particular methods of attack ?

There is first of all the General Strike. General strikes deserving of the name have been so few that it is almost possible in a study like this to list them all, and for once to be certain that at least our data are complete.

Pre-war general strikes differ in some respects from general strikes of to-day; nevertheless they have certain characteristics common to present-day strikes, especially in France, where the general strike was the workers' favourite (or at least most-discussed) weapon. The facts can be set out fairly briefly.

The first French general strikes of any importance were called in 1902 and 1903. Their objective was mainly to secure the closing of the private labour exchanges. As always in France, they were fought practically without funds. They were successful in their objective: but it is important to notice that their objective was strictly limited.

In the last-named year again, a strike call was issued to secure State support for technical education. How far it was answered is uncertain at this date. Some concessions were secured. In 1905 and 1906 calls were issued for strikes to secure the eight-hour day, and these resulted in no successes whatever. In 1909 the C.G.T. (*Confédération Générale du Travail*— the central French Trade Union organization) issued a call for a general strike to support the postmen, which was not replied to by the federation's members.

We ought to add to these the post-war French general strikes, for they continued essentially the pre-war character of French general strikes. The only general strike which attained proportions that would justify it claiming the title in other countries was the strike of 1920. This was fairly well answered, and extended outside Paris (a remark it is necessary to make in discussing French general strikes) but was easily broken by the Government, and in its fall threatened momentarily to extinguish the C.G.T. altogether. Of this strike it should be noted that the majority in favour of calling it was less than two-thirds: an old trade union rule-of-thumb that no grave struggle should be entered on with less than that majority was thus re-endorsed. It was the half-heartedness of much of the membership that was responsible for the completeness of the crash. Soon after, the disputes of the Socialist International and Communist International tore the French trade union movement in half and both C.G.T. and C.G.T.U. (the latter being the " Red " organization) clamoured for the allegiance of the French workers. Calls for a general strike were sent out, especially by the latter body, with extreme levity. Neither body would consent to co-operate with the other. When, as in 1927, in protest against the judicial murder of Sacco and Vanzetti, both organizations were agreed that a protest strike was necessary, they carefully fixed different days, as if to ensure defeat.

The leaders of the C.G.T. and the C.G.T.U. have succeeded in proving to the world only one thing—that the repeated use of the general strike for revolutionary ends does not end in shaking the capitalist system to pieces. It only results in enfeebling the unions, disgusting the workers with this particular weapon, and making the trade union leaders ridiculous.

In Belgium, before the war, the general strike was used three times, and with less inconsequence than in France. A general strike was called as early as 1893. The greatest astonishment was caused by this action. Its object was to secure universal suffrage. At the appearance of this phenomenon—so monstrous in those days—the Government gave way, and universal suffrage was granted, but plural voting was instituted as well. In 1902 and 1913 strikes were called to remove this undemocratic privilege. The strikes were far better organized and responded to, but they secured no concession. The Government serenely held to its course.

In other words, the Belgians discovered that the first general strike will, by the shock and terror of its novelty, extract quite surprising concessions from the governing class. But thereafter it is likely to extract nothing at all. The governing class knows the menace, and has had time to reflect that if it sits tight the workers will starve before the middle and upper classes, and will have to go back in defeat.

There was a general strike over a matter of Civil Service conditions in Holland in 1903. The strike was badly organized, and badly responded to; the workers were not interested in the objective proposed to them; and it has no lessons for us. The Swedish general strikes, on the other hand, have. In 1902 a three-day general strike was called against a Bill which would, effectively, have meant a large measure

of disfranchisement. It was magnificently successful;
the Bill was killed stone-dead. So far everything
seemed excellent. But there are other people than
revolutionary workers who can draw lessons from
general strikes. The Swedish employers were far
from pleased at this great display of strength by the
Swedish unions. They imitated and greatly improved
the unions' organization on their own side. In suc-
ceeding years they became more and more able to
fight the unions in isolated conflicts, and in 1909
actually used the general strike weapon against the
unions themselves. The market was falling heavily,
reductions of wages were being demanded everywhere, and the employers in general were quite
willing to see their factories closed down. The
Employers' Syndicate deliberately set out to harass
local units of the trade union Confederation until that
body was forced, by a wave of resentment, into calling
a general strike. Once they had secured this, the
Swedish employers held their factory gates shut till
the unions were shattered to pieces, and hard-won
agreements on wages and hours were consigned to the
waste-paper basket. The general strike as a weapon
had been successfully turned against its inventors.

But all these pre-war examples are, of course, of
trivial importance compared with the Russian
general strikes which in 1905 actually started an
unsuccessful revolution. There is no room here to
explain the circumstances which led up to the
October strike of 1905. It must be sufficient to say
that the Tsar's government was such that no especial

reasons need be sought for explanation of a revolt, but rather for explanation of quiet, and that the ignoble disasters of the Russo-Japanese war had made it especially vulnerable.

The first general strike broke out, apparently spontaneously, in St. Petersburg in October 17th. It spread rapidly. Large sections of the middle class, including doctors and lawyers, joined in. The objective of the strike was definitely revolutionary—it was the ending of the autocracy and the substitution of a constitutional monarchy. How far it spread outside the capital is uncertain: probably not to any great extent, nor was it complete within it. But it was very formidable, and the Tsar gave way before it. The strike ended on November 1st with the granting of a constitution.

The revolution of 1905 was now begun. The Tsarist government did not observe its promises, and a long and bloody struggle followed. The general strike was used twice more. Only a fortnight later Poland was excluded from the constitution. The strike committee (the Russian word for which, unnoticed then, is COBET, Soviet) called another strike. There was less general enthusiasm, especially among the middle class, because the object of the strike was less universally appealing; but the strike was far better organized. It lasted for five days. The minutes of the Soviet are extant. They show the strike extending to new areas and being maintained in the old. They show the Cossacks and police riding down and shooting the strikers, who have no means of self-defence. They show the Government merely standing aside and waiting. In the end, on November 19th, the Soviet called off the strike, without achieving its object, but having secured some prestige by the amount of strength that it had shown.

On December 20th the Tsar struck his return blow. The committee, headed by Chairman Trotsky, was arrested *en bloc*. The Socialist parties of all shades (there were no Communists then) sent out immediately a strike call. The St. Petersburg workers were disorganized, but Moscow came out. The railways stopped, and the Moscow garrison fought with the strikers. Almost at once the strike became an insurrection, which was fought and extinguished in the usual military manner. With its suppression was broken the effective strength of the revolution.

The general strikes which we have considered so far are practically all pre-war in date, and are all pre-war in type. We can, however, deduce already certain general principles. The first is, as we have said, that the *first* general strike will, by surprise, extract concessions that no later one will. The second is that a general strike, of the pre-war type, is like a riot or other means of inflicting discomfort upon the governing class and is correspondingly limited. Ultimately, if the discomfort that it causes is greater than the discomfort that would be caused by yielding to its demands, then the strike will be won. If its demands would cause graver discomfort than resisting it causes, it will be defeated. In practical terms, a general strike could secure, let us say, a rise in the rate of relief offered to the unemployed, or the abandonment of food taxes or other taxes which press particularly heavily on the working class. These are demands which could, albeit inconveniently, be granted by the governing class by means of budgetary rearrangements, without damaging its power. It could *not* secure any things which involve any actual abandonment of control—for example, it is highly improbable that even the best-organized strike threat would secure the control of finance, or even the control of any major industry.

Since the war, however, these examples of what might be called normal general strikes have been supplemented by turbulent outbursts which have occurred while governments and societies were tottering to ruin. Where general strikes have assisted in overturning them it has been very difficult to say that they would not have fallen anyway.

Two or three instances out of many, however, may be found showing as far as possible the post-war general strike acting in chemically pure conditions, so to speak—more or less isolated from other means of coercion. These are the anti-Kapp general strike in Germany in March 1920, the Italian anti-Fascist strike in August 1922, and the great British general strike of 1926. Perhaps equally significant was a general strike which never occurred at all—the strike call issued by the British Council of Action in August 1920.

In March 1920, perceiving the weakness of the

German Government, headed by the Social-Democrat Herr Bauer, two enterprising Junkers, Dr. Kapp and General Lüttwitz, Hitlers before their time, seized the Government in Berlin. Their storm troops were some six or seven thousand " Baltic " troops returned from the Eastern front, brutalized soldiers of the Black-and-Tan type who could be trusted to do any violence. Herr Bauer and his colleagues, expelled from Berlin, endorsed the calling of a general strike by both the official Socialists and the more intelligent and courageous Independent Socialists. The call was enthusiastically obeyed, and large numbers both of Catholic workers and of the middle class co-operated. Government officials in particular ignored the usurpers' instructions. Within two days the Kapp Government was endeavouring to make a compromise, within three it was in flight.

In these few days' limits the strike was grandiosely successful; but immediately following events were discouraging. The Independents and the official Socialists violently disagreed, and the growing Communist influence was thrown behind the former. Before long the victors in the general strike were at each other's throats. The Communists and Independents demanded a Socialist republic; the official Socialists, strangely enough, opposed this and insisted on a capitalist republic. They succeeded, after a bloody struggle, in their strange desire, and entered on the broad road whose far end was guarded by Hitler and Goering.

But these later events prove to us no more than that

I

those who lead a general strike should know why and for what they lead it; and we must be unusual fools to need a demonstration to prove that to us. We would be better employed in comparing the Kapp strike with the anti-Mussolini strike of two years later, which failed completely—or with the strike against Hitler which was never called at all. The Italian strike failed, and the German strike was never called, for the same reasons. Normally a general strike in defence of a threatened Republican, " Left," or Socialist government starts with an immense advantage. It is presumed to have the support of Government officials and the middle-class circles from which these officials spring. But in Rome and Berlin, in 1922 and 1933, these were absent. The Government officials were rotten with Fascism. The middle class, even the most enlightened, were exhausted by economic disasters and impatient with the fumbling uncertainty of the official Socialists. In times of despair they may be willing to make the icy plunge into Socialism. But no class, no body of persons, however patient, can for ever agree to wait about for years while a supposedly revolutionary party makes up its mind whether it will or will not carry its programme into effect. Sudden death, with the hope of heaven beyond, may be accepted, but perpetually deferred assassination no one can tolerate.

The second reason was that by that time the working class, on whom alone fell the duty of supporting the strike, was deeply divided. The Communist-Socialist split had sliced right through the working class. Men who have struggled for months as enemies cannot effectively unite at the last moment against an infuriated, well-armed foe. The local bitternesses, the rivalries in shop committees and trade union branches, are too deep and cannot be healed but by a number of personal reconciliations which take time. The German and Italian revolutionaries, in Lord Melbourne's phrase, did not hang together, so they were hanged separately.

The absence of such a split was the reason for the success of the British Council of Action in 1920. In that year the Poles had made an unprovoked invasion into Russia. They had reached as far as Kieff when the Russian army, freed from other entanglements, took them in hand seriously. The Polish army then ran, and continued to run for some hundreds of miles, until it began to look as though Warsaw would fall. If a Polish Soviet Republic appeared, then it was not at all unlikely, with Germany as disordered as she was, that the Soviet frontier might be advanced to the Rhine. The British and French governments entered into consultation to prevent this. A big expeditionary force, they considered, would undoubtedly paralyse the Russian advance. Munitions were already being sent out to the Poles. An Anglo-French conference was actually held at Lympne, to which Marshal Foch was called in. There was no doubt, in the minds of most working-class people, and for that matter in most other circles, that the expeditionary force was practically arranged for, when a spontaneous dock strike in London gave the signal for drastic action by a specially summoned council of union delegates. This body, assuming the name of " Council of Action," laid an embargo on all munitions and troop trains and threatened the Government with a general strike unless all war projects were abandoned. The effect of this threat was instant. The Government immediately abandoned its plans, and with uplifted hands protested that the thought of war was intolerable to it. French aid alone and a French military mission saved Warsaw.

Such an example is perfect of its kind, and perfectly convincing. No one need doubt henceforward that a general strike can stop a war, and that such a general strike can be organized. But even here there are conditions. Trade Union organizations must exist to make the threat. They must not have been stamped out as Hitler and Mussolini have stamped out their national organizations; nor must they be thoroughly rotted as some of the A.F. of L. organizations are rotted. There must also be either manifest aggression (as there was in 1920) or if the issues are confused, as they most probably will be, there must be reasonable hope of parallel action on the other side of the frontier. Concretely, one may say that British Labour would probably threaten a strike against a Government which proposed war on France or the United States. But would it seriously threaten such a strike against a war with Hitler which Hitler appeared to be asking for ? Probably not.

In any case, we are now considering not merely

stopping a war, but means of drastic social change. The biggest of all general strikes whose object was to compel a Government to a considerable change in internal policy was the British general strike of 1926. It lasted nine days, and in that short period of time raised and settled a surprising number of questions of tactics. In the first place it showed, as might have been expected, that a general strike is almost always a revolutionary act. Those people (and they were not few) who expected the strike to be a method of bringing pressure to bear on the coal-owners to prevent them reducing the miners' wages were undeceived the minute the clocks struck midnight on Monday. From that moment the coal-owners were forgotten, and the struggle was a straight issue between the State and the Trades Union Congress. The defeat of the employers would have meant the defeat of the State by the forces of Labour, and the political consequences of that are not easy to calculate, but they would have been immense.

And then, again, it was shown that henceforward no general strike need ever be general. Consider the tactics of Congress. Its first strike call was not a general call. It called out the following great blocks of workers: the railwaymen, the transport workers, the printers, the iron and steel workers and the builders. This call was followed, on the Tuesday of the next week, by a call on the shipyard workers and the engineers. But these categories do not at all exhaust the lists of the unions affiliated to the Trades Union Congress. There were whole blocks of workers, such as the textile workers, which nobody ever thought of calling out when the actual struggle came. They were not called out because their offensive capacity, in industrial warfare, is so small. Who cares, in a moment of crisis, whether the textile factories, the schools, and the musical-instrument factories are working or not? Their immediate controllers, and no one else at all.

Those who lived through the general strike will have realized that the same classification applied to the trades actually called out. Some of the strikers had enormous offensive power, some had scarcely any. The Government was hardly at all inconvenienced by the idleness of the builders, the iron and steel workers, and the shipyard workers. They served a purpose, indeed, but it was a minor purpose. Their numbers added to the enthusiasm: they could, as it were, swell the crowd and deepen the cheers. Any future strike-leaders will have to consider carefully the various trades and classify them according to their attacking capacity. Those which have little or no attacking power they will probably say had better stay at work and with their subscriptions feed those who have to bear the brunt of the battle.

The first class—those whose attack can seriously incommode the Government—appears to include, above all, all communications-workers—using the word " communications " in its widest sense. These are as follows: railroad workers; distributive workers; road transport workers; airmen and air transport workers; sailors; electrical workers; post and telegraph workers; dockers; radio-station workers; printing trade workers. The second class, whose abstention from work would only drain the unions' funds, probably include great masses of workers such as the builders, textile workers, miners, iron and steel workers and brewers. The position of the engineering trade is uncertain, and it is clear that for the limited period of harvest, farm workers, could they be organized, would have a great offensive power.

It was also made clear that a general-strike committee must be prepared with a policy for the control of food. The British Co-operative Movement provided a possibility of handling this problem which is not always likely to be available. But it was not effectively used: some " Co-ops " were unfriendly, and in others workers were marched in and out by contradictory orders. Even strikers and their families have to eat, and if elementary necessities are not provided by the striking authorities they will have to get them from blackleg sources. Friendly firms, of established trade union standing, were sometimes allowed to operate under licence, and town councils which were controlled by Labour majorities were able to co-operate with the strikers. These are agencies that might be used even where there is no Co-operative organization.

The circumstances of the end of the strike also have a definite lesson for future struggles. There is no point, here, in reviving ancient squabbles. One fact is at least agreed, and nobody's feelings can be hurt by mentioning it. At the end the Trades Union Congress made a certain agreement by which the miners declined to be bound, stating that they had not authorized the Congress to act for them. Consequently, they lost the benefits (if any) that the agreement had provided for them, and the Congress's followers discovered that their strike had been in vain. The strike and the lock-out both ended in dreary disaster. Nothing whatever was gained.

It is quite certain, whether or no the Congress was wise to call off the strike on the Samuel Memorandum, that no general strike should ever be conducted except by a body which had disciplinary powers, and is entitled to attack, defend, conclude peace, or make negotiations, on behalf of all its constituent bodies—especially that body in whose defence it is fighting. The whole army cannot possibly be held in the field because one regiment is dissatisfied with the terms. No one outside Bedlam could imagine anything else; and even if the ideas of Bedlam are still passionately defended in certain trade union offices that is no concern of ours.

We can already see certain objectives that should be aimed at by anyone who wishes to make an effective general strike more possible. We might list them as follows:

Control of the Co-operative Movement by intelligent and convinced revolutionaries.

Control of the local municipal bodies.

A central authority with power to say *Yes* and *No*.

Better organization of the trade unions, probably on industrial unionist lines.

Calling out of trade unions in accordance with a planned scheme based on their effectiveness.

Organization of certain dangerous " black spots," now untouched, like the radio workers.

All these are possibilities in some countries at least, including England. But even if they are secured, and our imaginary council has called a general strike, it is clear that a time will come when something more will be needed. If both sides remain with folded arms, the strikers will lose. They will starve before Whitehall or Washington does. And even if both sides wish to remain with folded arms events will not allow them to. The moment strike-breakers appear, violence will follow. There are bound to be events such as wrecking trains and spiking omnibuses. Probably not many governments will follow M. Briand's example of calling up the strikers into the army—it is too like arming your enemy. But the regular army can and will be used to prevent these disorders; and the moment this occurs you are straight into a civil war and your problems are those of a civil war (which we will consider later) and not those of a general strike at all.

Very possibly, skilled non-violence, or the skilled evasion of violence by the other side, might lead to the taking over, here or there, of one town or another, in the way in which large areas of Ireland slipped quietly into the hands of Sinn Fein before ever Mr. Lloyd George surrendered. According to some accounts, both Seattle and Winnipeg have since the war been in the hands of strike committees in such a way. But that is all, and it is very little. Nobody can, from the control of one city, Liverpool, Baltimore, or Medicine Hat, proceed to control a whole community and replan it as an organized whole. You must go forward to a national capture of power or else go back to the limbo where the Seattle and Winnipeg strike committees are to-day.

Such a national capture is exceedingly unlikely. Government offices are not built of sand, and will not fall down however wildly the turbid waters swirl round them. Always, after the conflict, there is likely to be standing a still-defended Whitehall, with police and soldiers at its orders.

Yet there are possibilities. Round about the Monday, for example, of the British general strike (the seventh day) there was clearly a potentially revolutionary situation. The other side was badly rattled, and its protection insufficient. At that time I remember a man, now an eminent and respectable Liberal, saying as he looked up at Big Ben: " If only we had a few hundred well-armed and determined men, the Government could be put out of existence right away." Perhaps he was optimistic; in any case the chance was only due to the confidence of the British Government that the British Labour movement was too respectable to attempt any such thing. But the nerve of the British Government was weakening (indeed, the last phase of the conflict was a race of galloping degeneration of nerve on the part of the chiefs on both sides) and was being weakened by the bellicose demonstrations that were held, by the remarkable solidarity shown and by certain small but definite signs of sympathy from the soldiers. If this at another time were to progress so far as to cause the Government to sue for a compromise, which was a real and not a fake compromise, a partial revolutionary victory would be secured. An event like this is not in the least inconceivable, though it would need high skill to secure it.

Such a compromise, to be effective from our point of view, must include in its terms the calling of an immediate general election—that is to say, it must involve the possibility of a change of government. An election is not, in recorded history, often a means of revolution; but an election immediately after a general strike is another matter. The forces of reaction are likely to be split by mutual accusations of cowardice, and the revolutionary votes will be swelled by the votes of those who always go to the apparently victorious side.

It is time we arrived at last at some conclusion. We may decide that a general strike, where conditions permit of one at all, is a possible but not a probable instrument of social change. It requires other means—electoral or military—to bring it to final success, and it is very difficult to manœuvre. It is, however, a very powerful means of preventing a war or defending an attacked government.

# CHAPTER VII

## FINANCIAL PRESSURE

THERE is one method of revolutionary change which is continually appearing in discussions and disappearing. It is the method of financial pressure. All capitalist business runs only because the money market acts freely. Stop it, and business stops as certainly as any general strike could stop it.

In 1832, this method was actually tried with success. The Duke of Wellington was put at the head of a government which intended to prevent the Reform Bill. Francis Place and Joseph Parkes, the chief Whig intriguers, printed and placarded all over London a poster saying " To stop the Duke, go for Gold." The effect of this was so terrible a run on the banks that in a few hours the Duke resigned. But this is a weapon that can only be used by the capitalist class, not against it, for the obvious reason that the capitalist class is the one that owns and controls money. It can be used for the defence of capitalism, as it was used in 1931 to throw down the second Labour Government in Britain, but it cannot be used for attack. People who speculate upon the effects of all the workers simultaneously withdrawing their deposits from the Savings Banks, the Post Office, and the ordinary banks, are wasting their time and our;. No one can, and no one ever could, so control the working class as to make such a manœuvre possible. To indulge in such dreams is to live in an imaginary world.

There is no need to say anything more about financial methods of causing a revolution.

# CHAPTER VIII

## ARMED REVOLUTION

REVOLUTION to the average man means only one thing. It means the splendour of the shouting and the pikes; noble deaths upon the barricade; the rattle of rifles and the cry of the dying; the broken and shaking notes of the " International " or the " Marseillaise " between the heavy thunder of the guns. Armed revolt is the traditional method of revolution, and it is very difficult to deny that hardly any examples of successful revolution by peaceful means are to be found in history.

An enormous number of examples of armed revolt are available for our study, and to mention them all would be utterly impossible. They are so many that at the end of last century, by rule of thumb and multiplicity of examples, it seemed that some sort of general policy had been evolved. There was a fair knowledge of street fighting technique, whose details vary from town to town, and whose general principle is to strike at the vital spots of the enemy. These in Blanqui's days were administrative centres and armouries; in Trotsky's they are electric stations, railways and telephone exchanges. There was one general principle which was, in a sentence: " Arm the revolutionaries—the workers—and disarm the existing forces." If this was not done, during or instantly after the revolution, defeat was certain; if it was, the return of the old régime was made exceedingly difficult. Blanqui's followers, in 1839, went from gun-shop to gun-shop looting, in order to fulfil the first half of this instruction. They were unhappily not able to attempt the second. All the revolutions of 1848 failed precisely from neglect of this elementary principle. The governments occupied their new seats and drafted constitutions. They accepted with a pleased bow the assurances of the devotion of the generals and admirals of the old régime, and left them and their officers undisturbed. The very moment that the reactionary forces were strong enough, the same admirals and generals, often by open force, expelled the revolutionary government.

In 1905, in Russia, as we have observed already, the general strike was enough to secure the promise of a constitution but not its observance. During the second general strike the strikers found themselves helpless before the arms of the Cossacks, and the strike had to be called off in defeat. The Soviet had omitted to arm, or could not arm, its supporters.

Even later examples show the truth of this. The German revolution in 1918 ignored this rule of thumb. It begged Hindenburg to stay at the head of the army, and it only in part removed Junker and Nationalist officers and officials. Certainly, its Reichswehr was only partly Nationalist, but a separate Republican organization (the Reichsbanner) was necessary to defend the Republic. In the end, there was no force which was both competent and willing to stand up to Hitler's Brown Shirts. When a struggle was threatened in Prussia, the same Bauer who had once broken Kapp by a general strike meekly left his office before the smallest show of force. " A man who gave up power," said Hitler, perfectly justly, " to eleven men and a lieutenant had no right ever to be in power at all."

The present balance of power in Spain turns exactly upon the same question. The Clericals test and question how far the Army and the anti-Labour Guardia Civil have retained their pre-revolution offices and sentiments. So do the Socialists. Seven thousand army officers have been retired: they are Royalists. But what are the remainder? They are probably not Socialists. The Guardia Civil has been restrained from breaking strikes, its previous duty. But it has not changed its personnel: its members put down their great green-clad hams among the proletariat in the crowded trains as arrogantly as ever, and sit stiff, with rifles and shiny hard black helmets, staring at their ununiformed neighbours. There is no effective Republican Guard.

But these two examples only prove that this old maxim is still valid for protecting a revolution which takes a period of years or months to unroll itself. It is not any longer a valid instruction on how to start and win a revolution. The members of the British or American working class cannot any more make a revolution by looting gun-shops and then storming Buckingham Palace or the White House. Such instructions are as out of date as manuals on pike-making and barricade building. When the author of this was editor of the official British Communist journal, he was visited by a survivor of the Paris Commune—a venerable and eager white-bearded old man named Chamon. He came to deliver an instruction, as from an experienced revolutionary. " Your Executive Committee," he said, " is betraying the workers. It is probably composed of espys. It is losing its chances. Perceive. I live in Kensington, near the Cromwell Road. What an expanse of road, and how suitable for barricades! All through the winter you have the most benevolent fogs, in which these constructions could be made at leisure. And there are working-class districts near from which could pour forth the revolutionaries. Yet the police walk undisturbed as ever. No orders have been issued! But consider how admirable is the opportunity, and how entirely unprepared the enemy. Ah, camarade, if it is but the lack of experience that deters you, I, I who speak to you, old though I am, will direct the building of the first barricade ! "

He left me, after I had promised to convey his views to the Executive. As he left, a whole past generation of revolutionaries seemed to vanish with him. Their tactics and their theories are no longer valid: they are only historical curiosities. Hyndman and Lenin sought to find examples from the history of the Commune and even of the great French revolution, but their endeavours were necessarily unsuccessful.

K

What has essentially altered the problem is chiefly the change in transport facilities, and the consequent greater powers of suppression which are in the hands of the authorities.

The conflicts between the Assembly and the King in France in 1789 to us read like the accounts of chess matches between Lasker and Capablanca. Each side takes an immense time to decide on its next move. They sit at the board, silently contemplating the pieces for months. Moves that appear to strike right at the heart of the opponent's forces, that threaten an immediate checkmate, remain unanswered for weeks while the King or the Assembly reflect on the matter. The action of the Assembly, for example, in meeting at the Tennis Court in defiance of orders, and swearing an oath not to disperse until it had put an end to the absolute monarchy—this was surely a direct thrust to the heart. How long would, say, the Reichstag have lasted in 1933 if its majority had had the reckless idea of offering such a defiance to Herr Hitler ? But King Louis XIV waited for weeks before taking any action about it. The reason was that Marshal de Broglie was away in the east of France and the time that it took to bring him in and to assemble reliable troops was very considerable. Meanwhile, the game had to be held up. Desmoulins, on his side, could discover the royal plot, announce it to the *faubourgs*, stir them up day after day, and after taking his time, capture the Bastille.

From 1789 to 1792, three years, there was a continuous see-sawing struggle between the King and the people, and nobody could have told an observer where the real seat of power was. The people marched on Versailles or on the palace again and again. If they were successful, the King made concessions. If they were not, they retired back to their *faubourgs* and thought the matter over, to return again another day. The " sections " met at their own chosen time, discussed their failure, and made a fresh attempt a little later. This process of " holding an inquest " on a defeated revolution was so successful that to this day Communists look to it as a valid method, regardless of the change in circumstances. But revolutionaries to-day cannot assault the government, fail, and retire undisturbed to argue over the defeat as if it were a golf match. They will find that overnight they have become hunted hares, with no opportunity to discuss anything. Their unions, if they have been able to bring the unions in, will be shattered and years of building up, maybe, wrecked overnight. The telegraph and the railway have enabled governments to make sure that only the smallest hiding-places are safe from it. The same causes, which are the roots of most of the complexity of modern life, have made it sure that the workers' organizations will be highly developed and not easy to restore after defeat. A primitive organization like a Paris " section " of 1792 is a body like a primitive organism in the natural world—with few powers, but yet very hard to kill. Its influence was limited, but it was exceedingly difficult to prevent it immediately re-forming after a defeat. The National Union of Railwaymen or the Brotherhood of Locomotive Engineers has far greater offensive power than the Section of the Cordeliers, but once defeated it would be very hard to build it up again. Modern conditions do not allow would-be revolutionaries to hang about and discuss their errors. In national wars decisions come slowly and after years of " war of attrition." There are no decisive sudden Waterloos. But in revolutionary battles the exact opposite is true: victory must be sudden or is irredeemably lost.

The latest of all examples of a proletarian insurrection occurred in Chile in 1932. Full details have not yet reached England, and those that have (such as the fact that the leaders of this Spanish-American revolt had Irish or Cornish names) are interesting rather than significant. But certain main lines of development are clear. Chile has long depended for its prosperity on the enormous deposits of nitrate in the north. A great corporation (Cosach), largely financed from abroad, had secured control of its output. The usual effects of the slump were intensified, here, by the discovery and exploitation of a method of artificially producing nitrate, which threatened ultimately to destroy the industry altogether. The ruin of Chile became a byword even in Europe. The Press printed stories of whole towns of 25,000 inhabitants, being literally sold as " scrap," because the means of livelihood had for ever departed from them. So complete a wreck and so sudden a decline from prosperity was bound to produce, and did produce, in the town working class and the farmers the sort of revolutionary ferment that is summarily described as " Communist." (There was, in fact, no effective Communist Party in control.) This ferment extended to the Army and particularly to the Navy.

A short inspection of the map will show that Chile, far more than any other country in the world, not excepting Great Britain, is dependent on the Navy. If the Navy goes " red," one would say, the question is settled. Chile is a long thin strip of land, lying between the Andes and the sea. There is no single town of importance that cannot be blown off the map by naval guns. A government which tried to stand up to a rebel Navy would have to take to the foothills, where it would starve in a month. So, one would have said, the revolt of the Navy should have meant the success of the revolution. But it was suddenly shown that communications had advanced a step further since the end of the war. The government hedged for a minute, long enough to call up the air force. The aeroplanes descended upon the confident Navy, bombed it from the air, rising and falling like birds of prey, and evading easily the clumsy showers of shrapnel from the anti-aircraft guns. Within a few hours the Navy had surrendered to one-twentieth of its number.

However, momentarily a happier ending was found.

*Pone seram, cohibe—*

wrote Juvenal:

> *sed quis custodiet ipsos*
> *custodes ? cauta est et ab illis incipit uxor.*

Which, freely translated, means that if a young woman is determined to go out on the tiles there is no good putting a male cousin to watch her: she will start with him. The revolutionaries promptly transferred their attention to the Air Force. The Red Flag which had been bombed off the ships was shortly floating over the aerodromes. The aviators turned on the government. They started off, in motor bus and taxi, oddly enough, to inform the President that he was dismissed. The motor buses, according to the news reports, broke down and only a small delegation arrived to see the President. He arose from his desk: " You are arrested," he said indignantly. " On the contrary, señor," they replied politely, " you are deposed." They explained to him the decision of the air force, and the hard truth enforced itself upon him. Facing some half-dozen travel-worn men, in a palace surrounded by loyal guards, he replied: " I surrender only to superior force: I shall go back to the farm."

Consequently, the Red revolution was for the minute victorious, though ensuing events were far too confused, and far too ill-reported for us to draw any further lessons.

But suppose the Air Force had not been amenable ? Suppose, as is quite conceivable in better-established countries, the government had seen to it that the air

force had only been recruited from the upper class ?
Then, so far from the revolution being victorious, we
see opening before us the prospect of a country being
wholly in the hands of a modern Prætorian Guard,
which can slay its enemies from the air, and be
immune from attack.

Let no one say, as answer to this: " The people
cannot nowadays be held indefinitely in subjection
by force." This is an article of faith, an assumed
axiom, with many people still; but it may simply
enough be disposed of by asking " Why not ? "
There is no reason. The powers of central authority
are more colossal than ever they were before, and yet
previous centuries are full of records of people submitting to the rule of force for vast periods of time.
Socialists, Republicans, Liberals, atheists and scientists are only men with lives to save and wives and children to fear for. If force is concentrated in a small
number of hands, and those hands use it ruthlessly
enough, they will abandon their opposition and
remain silent. For the small minority that does not,
there are large and modern prisons, and complaisant
doctors who will certify " instability of mind." The
political police to-day has more resources than the
Tsars, and there are few countries like the England
and Switzerland of last century, willing to shelter all
political refugees from some dim allegiance to a
principle of liberty.

Nor does a Prætorian Guard, such as the Fascists
led by Airman Balbo or the Nazis led by Airman
Goering, content itself merely with its own irresistible

force. Once in power, it sees to it that its victims like their subjection. No other but its own propaganda—directed in the crudest manner to glorifying both its leader's personality and the private army of Black or Brown Shirts that it relies upon—is allowed to exist. Men as a whole do not think connectedly and earnestly upon political subjects, and if only one set of ideas is legally permitted to appear before them, their opinions will be selected from that set and they will believe that they are exercising their free choice.

*Cauta est et ab illis incipit.* How shall the cautious revolutionary who fears, or hopes, that in armed revolt lies his only chance of success, deal with this last development ? The era of democracy began when the common archers shot down the noble knights at Agincourt and Crecy; has it ended when the gentlemanly air-fighter can defeat both Army and Navy ? How shall a revolutionary spread revolutionary feeling among flying men ?

There are three classes of aviators. There are, first, the officers and rank and file of the Air Forces. Generally, actual flying is only undertaken by officers, who are poor material for any but Fascist propagandists, and though the ground force is more hopeful, its power is very small. But the organization of support in the Air Force for a revolutionary *coup* is an integral part of the whole problem of the armed forces—the Navy, Army and police; and will have to be considered separately.

Let us consider the second two classes. These are the civil pilots and the private owners. The civil pilots are obviously organizable, as other workers are, into trade unions, and indeed at one time some of them in Britain held trade union cards. Were the trade union movement in earnest in its desire for change, it would be organizing them at high pressure now. But even when this was done—and it could be done forthwith—they are very few though very skilled. The machines they operate are chiefly heavy craft like bombers, and in a conflict similar to a new Paris Commune could rapidly be put out of action by fighters. As for the private owners, it is certain that the great majority of them are idle and adventurous rich men and women who are more likely to carry out raids against a struggling revolution than to fight for it. All that a revolutionary could say would be that it is the obvious duty of any well-to-do and earnest advocate of social change not only to learn to fly himself but to pay for the training of at least one class-conscious and reliable worker.

That, indeed, is a duty which, like the organizing of a union of pilots, lies upon the most peaceful as well as the most ferocious of those who genuinely desire a fundamental social change. For all these methods of influencing the opinion of airmen are as important to a strictly constitutional as to an insurrectionary government. No government, however impeccable its origin and methods, dare leave this tremendous weapon in the hands of its class enemies. Both Curragh and Invergordon, in their separate ways, showed that even the best trained and most loyal forces will, when strained beyond a certain point, refuse to obey orders, and must in the end be tied to the government by bonds of interest and sympathy. The Air Force may well be inimical to a reforming government; it must therefore, at the very least, be neutralized even by a most prudent and constitutional ministry.

Enough has now surely been said to show that one weapon must be wholly rejected from our arsenal. Direct armed revolt is no longer practical. But if that is true, it still does not mean that violence can or must be abandoned. Direct attack must fail, but indirect attack might succeed. Revolutionary propaganda could conceivably be turned like a jet upon the armed forces and the police, and it might be that concentration of energy here would prove a short cut to the revolution. Instead of revolutionaries fighting the Army, the Army might fight for the revolution. The tricks and deception of Parliamentarism would be avoided and, after all, the method is one that has commended itself to everyone in the past except the Victorian Liberals, whose dominance lasted but a very short time in world history. Certainly a man who imagines that men's opinions cease to count and should not be influenced or considered from the moment that they put on a uniform has a very fantastic view of politics.

Propaganda to this end is generally held to be illegal. The Communist International has always held this view, and in connection with it committed as early as 1920 one of its most serious blunders. It at that time published what amounted to the following short syllogism: " (a) propaganda in the armed forces is illegal; (b) it is also necessary for the revolution; therefore (c) we will admit no parties which do not promise forthwith to engage in illegal work." It acted, publicly, on that decision and made it binding on all constituent parties. Consequently it handed over all the Communist Parties outside Russia into the hands of the police whenever the police chose to round them up. They had no legal defence, and for the sake of revolutionary pedantry had abandoned the immensely valuable privilege of dodging in and out of the defences of bourgeois law in their struggles with society. It may be necessary—indeed very probably is—to break the law if you are earnestly intent on changing society. But one thing is quite certain, that if you propose to do so you should not announce the fact beforehand. No burglar calls the police when he is going burgling.

To what extent propaganda directed towards the armed forces is legal in Britain and the United States is very uncertain. Only a lawyer could say with any confidence what is legal and what is not; and he would probably be forced to add that his opinion, however well-documented, would no longer be valid in times of public excitement. One form of indirect propaganda is, I imagine, almost certainly legal, and it is surprising how little it has been used. The French and other revolutionaries have always forgotten a most important fact: that policemen and soldiers are chiefly working class in origin. They have assumed that the *flic* and the professional soldier are their natural enemies, and have consistently attacked them. Consequently, the police have become in fact their natural enemies, and war to the knife is a standing condition. But soldiers and policemen have wives, parents and sweethearts. These are of the working class, and know the conditions of working-class life and the sufferings that the present system causes. Their men who are in uniform cannot but be impressed by these facts, if only their relatives speak to them freely. They are, through the home, as susceptible as any others to the influence of the general economic causes that lead to revolutionary feeling. So much so is that the case that barrack life was instituted in the eighteenth century, not with any idea of military efficiency, but in order to remove the soldiers from " subversive " home influences and to make them more willing to shoot down the farmers evicted by the enclosures and the artisans starved by the industrial revolution. Any government which was genuinely democratic and did in fact rely " upon the people " would reverse this decision and abandon the barrack system. It would give its Army, Navy and Air Force members the necessary training, but allow them, like all other employed persons, to return home at nights. By such means alone could it secure that the armed forces would truly represent and defend the will of the people: this is the only means of preventing a Fascist *coup* or the domination of an officer caste.

Whether or no barracks can be abolished, it is fairly sure that they are not very likely to be abolished with capitalist and nationalist governments in power; that is a reform which is only likely to come after the revolution. In the meantime propaganda is going on, and a fair survey of advanced anti-militarist propaganda up to date must force upon us the conclusion that the greater portion of it is, whether legal or illegal, markedly ineffective. Strictly pacifist propaganda and strictly Communist propaganda are equally ill-directed, and up to date have been almost complete failures. This is so, because they take account of what the speaker believes to be absolute truth and not of what the audience is likely to be persuaded is true. The propagandists have failed utterly to follow the most important principle of modern advertising: that the customer is always right. Revolutionary propaganda addressed to the uniformed forces (or for that matter addressed to anybody) is merely sales-talk. The goods for sale are somewhat different from Listerine and Ballito silk stockings, but the method of approach must be the same. The vendors of mouth-washes do not suggest that their customers are ill-fed, under-exercised, spotty and unwashed young men, who smell disgusting and repel everyone who comes near. They present pictures of tall, well-groomed, handsome upstanding youths who are, with monstrous injustice, suddenly afflicted by a visitation of bad breath which can be removed only by using certain products. Silk-stocking merchants do not put out pictures of clumsily dressed, shambling young women with ill-fitting suspender-belts and sagging stockings: they draw slim graceful young things, full of sex appeal, who are chagrined and unjustly humiliated by ladders appearing on their divinely shaped legs— ladders which instantly (but without any blame to their possessors) drive away all eligible young men, and can forever be avoided by purchasing a different kind of stocking.

Similarly, pacifists who tell the uniformed forces that war is an abominable crime and that they are no better than murderers, and Communists who tell them that they are " imperialist lackeys and butchers," have absolutely no chance of a hearing. What they say may perhaps be true, but their audience can never be expected to believe it. Even soldiers and policemen whose general attitude is friendly will look round upon their good-natured colleagues and find that they look like neither murderers nor imperialist lackeys (whatever that may mean). No considerable body of men can ever be convinced that its whole occupation is vile. It may, in circumstances, be convinced that it has been tricked and caused to do wrong things; that is as far as it will go. Men may be willing to admit they have been fools, but not that they are knaves.

Any serious propaganda in any country where such propaganda was legal or tolerated would have to start by assuming that both soldiers and policemen perform useful functions and are not ignoble persons. It would differentiate between the various duties presented to them. It would agree at once to the valuable services of the police in traffic control, in running down murderers and stopping the drug traffic. It would admire their resistance to gangsters, and in particular their zeal in arresting white-slave traffickers and fraudulent financiers. It would stress the (presumed) desire of the average constable to protect the poor and needy; to aid the widow oppressed by rapacious landlords, to help home rather than charge the proletarian who has celebrated Saturday night too well, to turn a blind eye to unfortunates who break a law by having nowhere to sleep. It would, I expect, declare its belief that the Army existed only to repel a (hypothetical) predatory imperialist invader, and could not consent to be used against its own countrymen. It would thus suggest to the Army and the police that they were continually misused: that attacking the unemployed, chasing Communists or suppressing coloured nationalists are tasks which they should never have been asked to do —that, in fact, they were men of high character and courage who were continually misused and exploited by rich and greedy capitalists.

Persons in charge of such propaganda would discover that, like any other section of workers, uniformed workers will trust only those people who give real attention to their own special grievances, which vary from trade to trade. Labour members and trade union organizers, pamphleteers and reporters, would have to find what these grievances are and seek steadily to get them removed. For example, it might be found that policemen consider that they are deprived of elementary civil rights, such as the right of association, that their highest posts are reserved for imported military dug-outs, and are barred to the police, that their pay has been unjustly cut and that their discipline is often harshly and unintelligently enforced. Mr. Bernard Shaw, again, has long ago pointed out that soldiers have practically no rights under Army Law, are subjected to the rule of an absolutely alien caste, may be treated with personal violence, and are regularly set to senseless and childish routine tasks to keep them occupied. Skilled propagandists would raise questions such as these and agitate them continually, not as part of a " Don't shoot! " campaign, but as perfectly legal, parliamentary, constitutional agitation. At the same time, attention would be drawn to the class-character of enlistment to the high ranks, and an endeavour made to make sure that the services are genuinely open to all classes alike. (Incidentally, a task which the Trades Union Congress abandoned last century could well be resumed as well—the democratization of the legal machinery and the constitution of juries. At present all persons whose income falls below a certain level are deprived instantly of Magna Carta's privilege of being tried by their peers, and are consequently certain of oppression or of misunderstanding, or of both. This is an important means of suppression which might with certain concentration of energy be wrested away from the possessing class.)

When all this has been done, have we any real reason to hope that the uniformed workers will lead and make the revolution on behalf of the civilian population ? On the whole, probably not. Certainly, this has happened not infrequently in past history, and revolutions so made have not (contrary to general opinion) been the most bloody revolutions. But it has never happened at all, in any modern or highly organized state, except after a heavy defeat in war. The nearest examples which occur to the mind are Russia in 1917, Bavaria and Hungary in 1919, and France in 1871. There are no contrary examples whatever—no examples at all of an Army and Navy after a victory or in time of peace, turning upon the authorities and carrying through a social revolution. There was not even a real Fascist " march on Rome "—before the Black Shirt heroes started they made sure that the government in Rome had fallen into their power. And in these four examples, according to every account, the previous defeat of the Army was the sole thing which made the revolt of the common soldier possible. It shattered his faith in the courage and honesty of his officers, and made him think of them as enemies.

It is highly improbable, to say the least, that at any near date in the future the armed forces of Britain and the United States could be induced by even the most Machiavellian agitators to *turn on* their officers. And if revolutionaries offer themselves the hope that they might at least decline to obey orders to shoot and stand aside during a revolutionary attack, then they are still comforting themselves with pipe dreams. For, in order for such an abstention to be effective, it must be universal. If it is not, if an appreciable

L

number of armed forces continue to resist, the State is at once involved again in civil war, where chances of success, as we have seen, are slight. Even had the revolutionaries organized and ready to their hands a Blanquist army, what earthly hopes could they have that the gentlemen of the Guards and of West Point would fail to put up a resistance ?

We may surely at this point decide that the student of revolutionary technique must (subject of course to the appearance of extraordinary circumstances) conclude that armed revolt, as a method direct or indirect by a revolutionary *élite* or by a discontented army, is now totally impracticable.

Even to this statement, however, must be put a footnote. If his opponent holds most trumps, it still does not mean that the intelligent bridge player considers that all other suits are valueless. So an economical and well-directed use of violence may be valuable. It is very difficult for anyone who is not opposed to its use on religious grounds to deny this. The relatively good position of the French working class, for example, after the war was largely due to the fact that they had with reason secured the reputation of being dangerous people to meddle with. Very little else than the fear of exceedingly unpleasant personal experiences caused the French bourgeoisie to decide early to stabilize the franc at one-fifth of its pre-war value, which in effect meant that the cost of the war was to be taken out of middle-class savings instead of, as in England, out of the working class. In America, the A.F. of L. unions, those paragons of respectability in theory, have all through their history made a judicious use of violence, and frequently found that for individual unions it pays over quite long periods. All the world knows how, when the London unemployed in the great hunger march of last century smashed the club windows in Pall Mall, the Lord Mayor's relief fund was trebled in a few hours. It may have been charity, but it looked like fear, and the money was welcome. As late as 1922 apparently aimless violence like the attack of the unemployed on the Islington Guardians had a very clear effect in forcing the continuance of the dole.

Nevertheless, it must be admitted that this spasmodic and discreet violence has a strictly limited utility. Its use is confined by a formula similar to that which governs the use of the general strike. If concession to it causes less discomfort to the ruling class than resisting it, it will be successful; if not, not. The governing class will give in as far as it is reasonable to expect it to give in to avoid a row. You could—and the unemployed have before now—get increased relief by what the papers call " ugly scenes." But you cannot secure a revolution by bluff. You cannot, I suspect, secure the nationalization of even one industry.

# CHAPTER IX

EVIDENTLY, some of the most important suggestions about revolutionary technique ought to be discoverable in the history of the Communist International. This body has been engaged over a period of fifteen years in an organized international attempt to secure revolution. It has had considerable funds, a revolutionary citadel from which to operate, devoted adherents, sometimes at least a chance of the allegiance of the masses outside Russia, and the assistance of men of high intelligence, including Lenin, to guide it. All its operations have been carried on in the last decade, so there is no question of outmoded methods and ancient examples.

The Third or Communist International was founded in Moscow in 1919. Conferences were held, at first, every year. Later they were spaced out more, and at the time of writing no full conference has met at all for three or four years. During the years 1920 and 1921 large masses of the workers, inspired by the Russian revolution, were in a mood to consider joining the Third International. Conditions—including the once-famous Twenty-one Points—were put up which the existing organizations of the workers declined to accept. Among these was the

164

famous public promise to undertake illegal work, a romantic demand which seemed less melodramatic in Moscow surrounded by Red Guards than it did in Prague or Paris. These conditions afforded an admirable opportunity for the war-time, anti-revolutionary leaders of the Labour Movement to recover their lost prestige. The opportunity was taken, and as a result of these three years of struggle the mass of the workers did not, as was hoped, support the Communists, or form the necessary " mass-revolutionary " organizations. In every capitalist country almost without exception there were in 1922 old-style trade union movements in which the Communists had been deprived of all influence, and (occasionally) " red " trade unions which were relatively insignificant. Politically the working class was split into two parts. In most countries the Socialist Parties had an undeniable and marked superiority over the Third International parties; where this was not so, as in France, the ensuing years put the Socialist Party back into a commanding position. Large numbers of workers were continually throughout the next ten years attracted into the various Communist parties, but, in general, still larger numbers left them. The British Communist Party, for example, which started with 10,000 members, had in 1932 apparently rather less than half that number. (One says " apparently " because exact and reliable information about Communist parties is no longer given to the workers: estimates have to be used.) A very much larger number than ten thousand had passed through the Communist organization. " If the ex-members of the party " it was stated in London in 1932, " were laid end to end, they would reach from here to Moscow." The general line of development in the years 1922 to 1933 was, as is not denied by anyone, for Socialist (anti-revolutionary) organizations to recover their strength at the expense of the Communist or Communist-controlled bodies. One very considerable exception to this rule was to be observed. In Germany, after an initial recovery by the Social-Democrats, they appeared to be losing ground steadily to the Communist Party, which seemed to be on the way to becoming the mass party of the German workers after all. This tendency was becoming more marked in 1933, when both parties were overwhelmed by the Nazis and further development stopped.

No successful revolution anywhere has been conducted by the Third International. Two short-lived revolutionary governments were formed in 1919, in Bavaria and Hungary. They came to sudden ends and were in any case not directed by the Third International, which was not then organized. In 1927 a joint revolutionary enterprise by the Communist International and the Chinese Nationalist party, called the Kuo-min-tang, had spectacular successes immediately followed by a crushing defeat for the Communists when Chiang Kai-shek, the Kuo-min-tang General, turned upon them. Since then a reputed Soviet movement, of which nothing is known, has appeared in the interior of China.

It remains true, therefore, that the record of the Third International is one of failure. It set out to achieve world revolution; it has not achieved any revolution at all anywhere. However much chagrin this judgment may cause to earnest workers, it is impossible to sustain any other verdict. We can no longer inquire: " Has the Third International failed ? " but only: " Why has the Third International failed ? "

If such an inquiry is seriously conducted it is bound by implication to censure the Socialist leaders who did not even attempt to make a revolution. It will be even more resented by members of the Communist International, which since the expulsion of Trotsky has not permitted any serious difference of opinion, and whose members receive any criticism of existing leaders with a violent vituperation which very probably originates from a distrust in their own cause.

But words kill nobody, so let us proceed.

The first mistake of the Communist International lay in its constitution. It is a centralized body. It is one international party divided for administrative reasons into national units; not an international union of various national parties. All its members are controlled and directed (theoretically at least) by the " presidium " in Moscow, which again is ultimately responsible only to an international conference, when that meets. The conference decides policy, but that policy is interpreted by the presidium, whose instructions are binding on all members, including the executive bureaux and committees of the national parties. Individuals may be punished by the International, though that is of course rare; but the intention and effect of the international discipline is more to enforce all parties and all national executive bodies to follow exactly the lines laid down by the presidium and to suppress at once any " deviations."

The argument for this form of organization is that, because capital is internationally organized, labour to fight it must be organized internationally, too. At first sight this seems plausible, and is in a limited sense true. Labour movements with no international connections would be gravely hampered. But in general it is not true, it is only plausible. First of all, capital is *not* internationally organized. Only certain branches of capitalism are, and those very imperfectly. Furthermore, even in the world of capitalism international organization has in many important respects recently receded before increased nationalism. It is certainly still true that the greater number of the workers' struggles, trade unionist or political, have to be fought out nationally and not internationally. Secondly, even were this statement true, the deduction that Labour must be organized internationally in the Communist manner does not follow. So far from this strict and rigid discipline enabling the workers to fight their enemies it excludes precisely those swift-minded and independent workers whose allegiance is necessary. In any revolutionary crisis international control is a ludicrous idea.

Orthodox Communists should consider what would have happened in Russia from March to November 1917 had Lenin and his colleagues been under the discipline of an International. As it was they varied their tactics with the greatest speed and on most fundamental matters, passing in a few weeks from trying to ally themselves with the Mensheviks to trying to shoot them down. They demanded the calling of the Constituent Assembly as soon as possible and then closed it up when it came. They took charge of an insurrection in July, lost it, and tried again. But all this time they considered themselves members of the International, or at the very least of the anti-war section of the International. How on earth could they ever have succeeded in their task if they had had to obey the orders of an International committee sitting outside Russia and consisting of, say, Eugene Debs, Branting, Turati, Merrheim and Ramsay MacDonald—or whomever else you please ?

That such a prospect could be entertained at all as a plan for a future revolution, by reasoning beings, only shows that its defenders are living in a dream-world in which their International is such an organization as never could exist, directed exclusively by new and younger Lenins, who add to his energy and intelligence a miraculous knowledge of conditions and problems everywhere in the world. Any international revolutionary organization which may be built in the future must have powers of discipline, without question. It must retain the right to expel a party for counter-revolutionary activity (or inactivity) or aims. But such a right must only be exercised by a conference, after fair inquiry, and it is wholly impracticable to think of directing national party activities, in any but the most general way, from an international centre. People who accept the task of leading a movement for social change in any one country must take the responsibility for their own decisions and answer for them to those who have to carry them out and to suffer the consequences. If they will not, if they want a distant committee to advise and control them, be sure they are wholly unfitted for their positions.

Unwise in itself, this central authority was unwisely used. When the first Communist International Conference met in Moscow in 1919, there was no sort of uniformity to be seen among the bodies attending it, nor among those who were attracted to it and its satellite bodies in the next year or so. These organizations had, often, great vitality and glorious traditions of their own; they were overshadowed but not crushed by the Russians. There was the Italian Socialist Party, the I.W.W., the Spartakusbund, and later the German Communist Labour Party (K.A.P.D.—practically a Blanquist party), the Norwegian Labour Party and others. The Communist International deliberately set out to enforce uniformity upon them, as a considered policy. All their historic names were to be thrown overboard—no title was to be allowed but " the Communist Party of ——." Political organization had to be exactly the same, based on the Russian, with *politburos* and *agitprops* and all, regardless of whether the conditions called for them, and regardless, too, of the opinions of the local proletariat to whom these grotesque names were often either perplexing or the subject of disrespectful jokes. Political programmes had to be identical; so had economic and political " slogans," which meant naturally that they became so general as to be nearly devoid of meaning.

That this policy was right appeared to the Communists to be proved by the fact that the stronger organizations, which resisted it, came to bad ends. The K.A.P.D. passed out of existence. Mussolini massacred the Italian Socialist Party. The Norwegian Labour Party split. The I.W.W. withered up. The Communist International surveyed the ruins and, in manifestos which unfortunately became far more verbose as time went on, pointed in effect the nursery moral: " This comes of not doing what you're told."

But that that was so is exceedingly improbable. At least as fairly, blame may be laid upon the Third International for failing to accommodate its policy to the prejudices and traditions of working classes which had had different experiences from the Russians. It thereby had part responsibility for disasters like the Fascist revolt in Italy, in which, incidentally, its own " correct " organizations were annihilated as utterly as the " incorrect " ones. But this and other splits did not impress Mr. Zinovieff and his colleagues that way. They considered that they were entitled to assume, according to Marxist economics, that the capitalist crisis would grow worse and worse, and that more and more workers would consequently be driven into the Communist ranks. They felt that they could ignore, or treat as paid agents of the bourgeoisie, all those national labour leaders who hesitated or bargained about conditions of admission to the International, or of " discipline " once they were inside. Not less but more uniformity, not less but more ordering from the centre, was their remedy. The failures so far did not mean, they considered, that the medicine was bad, but that double doses should be taken. They felt that time worked fast and inexorably for them: they imagined the workers clamouring at their international gates, and, like good showmen, raised the price of admission.

But economic development cheated them. The promised flood of workers into the Communist parties prepared for them never came. From about the end of 1923 to the middle of 1928 capitalism stabilized itself. The workers' living conditions steadied, and sometimes even improved. So far from the revolutionary urge increasing it declined rapidly. The Communist International publications of those years angrily denied the fact, but events were too strong for it. The workers did not knock for admission at their doors: on the contrary, those who were inside began to leave. The International in disgust abandoned the *embourgeoisé* workers of Western Europe and America for the Far East, where misery was eternal.

Nevertheless, under the influence of their visionary hopes, Mr. Zinovieff and his colleagues had made their final and most serious blunder. This was the adoption of the policy of " bolshevisation " in 1923. It is impossible to understand this policy unless we remember that the presidium members had convinced themselves of the inevitability of a vast world-wide swing of the workers towards themselves. They believed, under this delusion, that they could regard the words " worker " and " Communist " as almost interchangeable: they could at least act as though all workers very soon would be either Communists or sympathizers. They could not, indeed, deny that there were in fact some who were not, but they regarded them as ripe fruit about to fall. Outside the parties they saw not (as was the case) the majority of organized and conscious workers, but a small minority of deliberate traitors and a number of fooled and backward followers. The latter were to be quickly brought up, as a crammer brings up a class of morons, to the general level by the use of what were called " lower organs," meaning small journals, local meetings and leaflets. " It is the duty," the Third International instructed the British Party, " of the lower organs of the Party to penetrate the backward parts of the proletariat." The former were to be regarded as enemies of the workers and extirpated by all the devices—including conspiracy, untruthfulness and dishonesty—till then reserved for the capitalist class.

To enable this to be done all Party members were

put under an exact control and personal discipline which was derived far more from Bakunin than Marx. Its name, bolshevisation, and historical justification were, however, taken from Lenin's famous conflict with Martov, which split the Russian Socialists before the war into Bolsheviks and Mensheviks. Martov wished to keep within the Party members who merely accepted the Party programme and paid their subscriptions. Lenin, with a greater perception of the reality of political conditions in Tsarist Russia, replied that no man should be allowed to belong to the Party who was not a worker for the Party—who did not in ascertainable fact put himself at the orders of the Executive, regularly and unceasingly and do reliably the work allotted, whether it was dangerous, or disgusting, or dull, or all three. There were to be no passengers, even if they offered money for their tickets. Lenin's plan was victorious, and Zinovieff transposed it to western conditions twenty years later without realizing that the circumstances were very different.

Certain considerable successes were achieved by bolshevisation. Serious revolutionaries do not want to be passengers, and if only they could be assured that discipline would be applied equally, and that their officials could be trusted, they were willing enough to take orders. Some at least of the membership that was squeezed out at first by " bolshevisation " was in fact little more than water. Those who remained showed a sudden increase of energy. They stood in the rain to sell Party papers, they came first and left last at open-air meetings, they affronted the police and interrupted rival Labour meetings with the patience and obstreperousness of the early Quakers. For all their small numbers they were deep and sharp thorns in their rivals' sides.

But as bolshevisation progressed it began to do more harm than it had done good. In the first place the new discipline became odious to the membership. It had been accepted by the pre-war Bolsheviks because the political conditions of Tsarism enforced it. Under terrorism such organization is necessary and the workers agree to it, but not otherwise. Perhaps it would be better if they did, but we have to deal with the imperfect material that human beings are. And in America and England, despite the oppression that does exist, the workers are not in fact living under a terror, though to this day the large majority of Russian Communists believe that they are. Membership figures fell, yet so far from slackening the discipline the International intensified it. Cross-examinations concerning members' private lives and activities were first permitted, and then compulsory. In Russia a " party purge " exists, in which a member is required to expose to his fellow members his soul and his relations with other persons. Cases are known in which members have been compelled to quarrel with relatives of unsuitable views as a price of retaining membership. Such extremes were not reached in England and America, but long steps were made towards them. I have myself, as a member of the Party, witnessed the cross-examination of a low-paid and semi-skilled engineer as to the way in which he spent his private time. He was able to prove that on Saturday afternoon and on every evening but one he was occupied either blamelessly or on Party work. " But what," said an accuser, springing from the second row, "do you do on Wednesday night ? " Had he been a Russian, it may be that our engineer would have delightedly seized the opportunity to expound the perplexities of his sex-life and the troubles that attend a worker who doubts if he has the money to take a deviating young woman to the pictures. But being of another race, he turned purple and advised the audience loudly to find itself a less (but not much less) indecent occupation than nosing into his affairs. His suggestion was ruled out of order, and within two days he had left the Party and with him a number of his friends. All over the country similar and little less foolish scenes were occurring, and the reluctance of members to accept this inquisition was enhanced by a distrust of their officials as " yes-men," which began to appear about the same time.

As bolshevisation proceeded, its ravages became more severe. Heresies were found with a facility and ingenuity that only the Early Church could rival. What are Brändlerism ? Zinovieffism ? Lovestonism ? Loreism ? What is a leftward deviation from the proletarian ideological norm ? I doubt if even the most " bolshevised " " monolithic," " in-the-line " Leninist Communist could say offhand now: yet they are real heresies, and numbers of people have been expelled for holding them. None of these terms have been invented by me.[1] The parties continually peeled portions of themselves off and threw them away, as if they had turned into onions with suicidal mania. This " onion-process " is not a rare symptom among revolutionary parties, from the Jacobins onwards, but any student of revolution recognizes it as a disquieting sign of grave disease.

The process of argument which identified " worker " with " Communist " also identified " non-Communist " with " class-enemy." The method to be used against all class enemies under bolshevisation was that of secret conspiracy. But, in Britain and the United States at least, it lamentably failed because of the impossibility of preserving secrecy. So many of the Communist workers failed to realize that their lifetime friends were now treacherous enemies, and " spilt the beans " from mere *naiveté*, while those that did were often too clumsy to conceal their manœuvres. At one meeting of the London Trades Council, of which the late Duncan Carmichael was secretary, a number of " spontaneous resolutions of revolt " were moved by delegates apparently from all over London. Their

[1] Not even the word " monolithic," which is genuinely a word of praise coveted by orthodox Communists. It is not, as an etymologist might think, Russian for " bonehead." It means " member of a party without any divisions of opinion in it."

M

common complexion roused Mr. Carmichael's curiosity, and he asked for the resolutions to be handed to him in writing. Each spontaneous delegate then presented him with a thin slip of typed paper, typed by the same machine, and when the slips were laid together their irregularities exactly fitted and they formed one foolscap sheet of paper.

This method of work was known as nucleus work—" nuclei-ing " was the term preferred by the then organizer. Its operation may be studied perhaps best in an organization like the then Labour Research Department, which the Communists desired to capture from the existing staff. The method was to arrange speakers and resolutions on committees beforehand, without the other workers knowing, in order that they might be swept away by what appeared to be a spontaneous outburst of energy, but was in fact a secretly rehearsed piece of acting. The first problem in this particular case (November 1923) was to pack the necessary subcommittees so that all the more important publications should be handed over to Communists, the second so to thwart the secretary, Mr. G. D. H. Cole, that he would be vexed into resigning. A " nucleus meeting " was called in November 1923 prior to the meetings of the Finance and General Purposes and Publications Committees, and the following orders as to behaviour were sent out to those absent from or present at the meeting. They are actors' parts, with cues: the initials represent other actors in the know:

261

*Decisions of meeting on* 14/11/23 *calling for action at F. & G. P. Com. on* 16/11/23 *or Publications Com. on* 20/11/23.

| DECISION | MOVER OR REPORTER |
|---|---|
| Co-options to E.C. M. H. D. | R. P. A. to get Cole to move. Otherwise A. L. B. |
| O. E. B. | E. B. |
| M. E. B. | R. P. D., R. W. P., or A. L. B. |
| Co-option to P. C. C. P. D. | E. B. |
| Labour & Capital Sub-C'ee. Move reappointment of R. P. A., E. B., M. E. B., R. P. A. | R. W. P. or R. P. D. |
| Syllabus Sub-C'ee. Move appointment of R. P. A., O. E. B., C. P. D., R. W. P. | E. B. |
| Postponement of E. C. | R. P. A. |
| Fourth Fridays for P. C. | R. P. D. or E. B. |
| Labour Party Pamphlet | Draft to be submitted by R. P. A., on report of his offer. |
| Studies | R. P. A. to report first on those arranged, traffic, building, cotton, coal. E. B. to raise question of single authorship. |

| DECISION | MOVER OR REPORTER |
|---|---|
| | R. P. A. then to propose authors for above four, H. P. R., H. P. R., E. B., Parsons, respectively. |
| | R. P. A. then to bring up proposed list of further studies, with authors, as follows. |
| | Iron and steel, M. P. P.; distribution, Pountney; soap, J. T. W. N.; tobacco, D. T.; agriculture, E. B.; oil, R. P. A.; and possibly also banking, M. H. D.; insurance, H. P. R. |
| | Cole to be fought in favour of Parsons-Rathbone draft of coal study with reference to sub-c'ee on that basis. |
| Year-book. A. L. B. as Editor. Offer of Local Govt. to Cole. | R. P. A. or E. B. |
| Syllabus Series. Move reference to sub-c'ee. | E. B. |

The writer of this book remembers how, on receiving a previous specimen of these instructions

marked " strictly secret," he suggested to the group
leader that it was unwise to send most secret material
through the post. He was answered: " Perhaps it
was unwise. But it is not very serious, for, you see,
it is not so much the police we wish to keep these
things secret from as from other members of the
Labour movement."

Such tactics could only be successful if the Communists' rivals had been in fact idiots led by scoun-
drels. But they were not: they were mischievous
beasts who defended themselves. They fought back:
and as it was the more left-wing bodies which the
Communists tried to control, it was precisely their
nearest allies which they found themselves attacking.
The present writer vainly endeavoured to prevent
the British Communist Party following this policy,
urging it to consider that it was digging a deep ditch
between itself and its closest fellow workers; and on
his advice being rejected withdrew from the Communist Party. Nothing that has occurred since has
caused him to change his mind. With the adoption
of this policy the Party finally ceased to be a possible
instrument of revolution. It filled the minds of the
most energetic and independent workers with hatred
and distrust of the Communists. It gave them as
enemies not men like J. H. Thomas, Ramsay
MacDonald or John Lewis, who might reasonably be
considered to have abandoned their original tenets
altogether and to have gone over to the other side,
and whose enmity might perhaps be considered a
compliment. It embroiled them with precisely the

patient and courageous rank-and-file workers who kept alive locals and branches in the face of capitalist persecution in industrial towns and mining villages, and who were most liable to find their organizations and themselves " captured " by a " revolutionary cell." It made even some strong revolutionaries regard the name Communist as the equivalent of crook and liar. At the Labour Party Congress of 1933, when the question of the " united front " should theoretically have come up, it received no consideration. But this was not because corrupt reformist leaders stamped out a rank-and-file revolt. They had no need to: it was the delegates of local Labour parties, unspoiled workers, who had had so large a bellyful of Communist tactics that they would not, for however just a cause, associate with them.

While this grim hatred—continually damped down by the necessities of capitalist life and continually fanned by the follies of bolshevisation—was burning, the Communist parties were faced by an impossible task in endeavouring to represent the workers as a mass. They had, in all countries, a formula of an identical kind. It has never worked in any single country, but they still adhere to it. It is: " The workers must support the reformist Socialist and trade union bodies for a time, in order that they may be disillusioned by their treachery while in power; they will then turn to the Communist Party." In fact, the fruits of this policy have always fallen into Fascist and never into Communist laps. There have been Socialist victories enough, in Britain, Italy,

Germany and Spain, and often there have been cowardice and inertia sufficient to deserve, if you so wish, the name of treachery; but the second part of the prophecy has never been fulfilled. In attempting to operate this policy the Communist parties were compelled to say entirely opposite things at the same time. They had to urge, in England, for example, the workers to support the Labour Party, because it was despicable and would betray them. T. A. Jackson, one of their leading theorists, disclosed this essential contradiction in a flaming speech which induced the Communist Party to apply for affiliation to the Labour Party. " Let us take the Labour leaders by the hand," he cried, " in order later to take them by the throat! " Even had not the Labour leaders callously refused this embrace, the Communist Party would before long have been hideously embarrassed by having to interpret its own slogan. Trotsky, at that time still the premier theorist of official Communism, provided a specific instruction which, more than anything else could, shows the freakish absurdity to which Communist tactics had arrived. The Communists, he said in *Where is Britain Going ?*, should relentlessly expose from day to day the servile treachery of the Labour Party lackeys, and also demand that the trade unions expel any members who failed to pay the political levy to support the aforementioned lackeys. No working class, no class at all, can possibly answer the cry: " Rally to the support of those who will betray you! Vote for your enemies, Thomas, MacDonald, and Henderson, that

you may have the full experience of their meanness
and treachery towards you!" Nor has the *Daily
Worker* in England secured any considerable response
for its economic campaign; for the worker who can
read from one column to the other can easily put
together the astounding clarion call: " Come out on
strike! If you do, your leaders will instantly sell you
out!"

However true such a cry may be, it has not spread
revolutionary feeling; it has spread rather what the
French call *je-m'en-foutisme*. Communist propaganda
has induced the workers to distrust their political and
economic leaders; Communist activity has caused
them to dislike the Communists. The net result has
been to produce that disillusioned and cynical state
of mind (most of all favourable to Fascism) where the
working class is imbued with a belief that all action
must necessarily fail; and all proposals, even for the
most useful and hopeful action, are greeted with the
equivalents of " however thin you slice it, it's still
boloney," or merely " ——! and the same to you!"

# PART IV—CONCLUSIONS

## CHAPTER X

### SOME SUGGESTED ACTION

Up to the present the writer has conscientiously endeavoured to maintain an absolutely detached mind. He has tried to suppress wholly any feelings he may have had of repulsion to certain methods—such as those of private assassination—or of affection to others. How far he has done this he does not know: he can only protest that his intentions have been completely honest. But he has not endeavoured to reach this detachment from a pure love of abstract knowledge, or because he has no strong interest in the subject under discussion. Far from it; he has the most passionate feelings upon it, and would not have entered on this study if he had not believed that his own dearest hopes and the ultimate happiness of millions were not endangered by loose thinking on methods of social change.

Looking over what he has written, he finds nothing that he would wish to change, now that the time has come to draw a conclusion, except perhaps to stress rather more the increasing power of the " technician " in modern industry. Rationalization, and the consequent growth of machinery and standardized production, has meant the appearance of a floating army of unemployed in every modern society which is greater than ever before. This in its turn means that the once-powerful proletarian armies, the unions of miners, ironworkers, transport-workers and so forth, live under a permanent shadow. Their fighting power is sensibly diminished by the menace of that vast reserve of helpless men who will, sooner or later, be willing to become blacklegs. Consequently, rather greater power than before is concentrated in the hands of a relatively small number of technicians who can cause to work, or make to cease working, many vital and profitable industries. Any movement for social change, therefore, must rely somewhat more on them than it has done and adapt its propaganda accordingly.

After this footnote has been written, it is necessary to draw some deductions about immediate action, and it is no longer possible for the writer to be impartial. Let those whose interest is purely abstract read no further: the time has come for a definite statement of personal wishes and conclusions. It should run as under:

I have written this book definitely as a member of the Labour Party. I am not in the least (and I think no civilized being is) interested in " the revolution " for the sake of revolution. I think that an outburst of civil violence which serves no further purpose than to liberate the sadism of middle-class Nazis or working-class toughs or aristocratic debauchees is possibly the most hideous and destructive social event that can be imagined. I only consider methods of revolution because I am firmly convinced that unwillingness to allow for unpleasant facts (as in Germany) leads us directly into just such a barbarous phenomenon.

I care only for a fundamentally democratic and libertarian change. I am prepared to make sacrifices only for a society in which all men shall be equal, in which all can be assured of a good livelihood, and in which no man can say to any other man (and no man to any woman—and no woman to any man): " You shall do this because I order you to." I hate the tyranny of class, based on money or heredity, first of all; I hate in the second place the tyrannies based on sex distinction and on religion. Because of this I am a Socialist and a member of the Labour Party. To those who agree with me in these opinions I wish to offer certain deductions from this study: others will not be interested in them.

With this preface, I would like to offer the following entirely tentative suggestions. I think we might well concentrate upon inducing Socialists to abandon some of the subjects which are generally discussed at conferences and endeavour to secure a collective agreement and will to some ends like the following:

1. That the next Labour Government shall hold on to office as firmly as Stalin's or Mussolini's—that it shall not quit until it has founded a Socialist State so firmly that an appeal to the electorate is quite safe. It should not be jumped into an election by any campaign, however ingenious. Its job

should be to " make Socialism "—it should fight one election on that issue and then not leave office until it has completed that job.

2. It should control radio broadcasting and other forms of propaganda, including the Press. The existing Press is corrupt, as it depends upon the will of advertisers. Once the chief revenue-paying industries are in State hands the Press will give no more trouble; for its proprietors and editors are not men with passionate convictions about freedom of speech, they are servants of money or owners of it.

3. It should secure forthwith, by the necessary reforms, the genuine support of the ranks of the services, including the police, and it should remove swiftly any technical constitutional obstructions, such as the House of Lords in Great Britain.

4. It should be prepared to offer an immediate palliative to existing sufferings; for example, a scheme of work for a million and a quarter unemployed.

5. In a country such as England, where foreign intrigue might lead to a threat of starvation, it should accumulate food-stocks, and grain in granaries.

These proposals are not new, and obviously could be extended, amended and elaborated. But it is quite certain that no individual effort is going to secure a Labour Government which is likely to do these things. Organization is needed. What sort of organization ?

Three things have resulted from our inquiries:

1. Armed insurrection is an unlikely instrument of change to-day.
2. A general strike is an unlikely instrument of change to-day, though it is serviceable in two other ways. It can *probably* prevent a war, and almost certainly save an established government from a counter-revolutionary *coup*.

These two observations may not be true after a war. After a war armed insurrection may be possible and a general strike may put down a government. But we have seen that the effects of a war are incalculable, or so far as they are calculable, seem to point more to the destruction of all organized society than to anything else. Certainly, not the most rigid Communist has as yet had the hardihood to advocate provoking a war in order to have a revolution afterwards.

3. The only remaining method is consequently constitutional Parliamentarism, and this constitutional campaign must be directed by a genuinely determined headquarters.

How on earth can this be secured ?

It is obvious, from the examples which we have turned over—the specimens in our revolutionary museum—that the big parliamentary organisms, the Marxist, Labour or Socialist parties become easily enough " mass organizations "—quantity organizations—but lose in that process the concentration of energy necessary to make a revolution. Other, smaller Blanquist or Anarchist, bodies secure the energy and become " quality organizations," but by their very nature seem unable to gain mass support. Apparently the dilemma is complete. But this only means that we must discover, or if necessary invent, a body which will combine the attributes of both types.

In Great Britain, the United States and perhaps Spain, such a task is not impossible. In countries where there are already strong, bitterly hostile Socialist and Communist organizations, the task is far more difficult. But in the first two countries at least the great mass of the working class is not yet split into totally separate parts. In the United States there is no mass Socialist organization at all. The Socialist Party is tiny, and the workers as a whole are floating loose, without political affiliations other than the weak tie of Republican or Democratic sympathies. The only organization of a " mass " character is the American Federation of Labour, which has been inflated by a sudden rush of workers under the New Deal. What effect this sudden infusion of new blood will have is not yet known. Old-style A.F. of L. unions were obviously useless. But others, like the Amalgamated Clothing Workers, have not abandoned their trade union activities, and if ever the American workers enforce a drastic social change, could be induced to take their part.

Within—so long as it is within, and not outside, shouting denunciations from a Communist fortress— within a working class which is either unorganized or adheres to a loosely organized body, a society of men such as the Bolsheviks were in 1917, can take the lead and direct a revolution. But these men must not come in from outside and expect their fellow workers to take orders from them. The personnel of such a body can only be made up of people who are already working within the movement and have secured and deserve the allegiance of their fellow workers. They must most certainly not expect to reserve for themselves the " brain-work " and other attractive jobs: with or without reason the working class will not entrust itself to an *élite* with soft hands and good intentions.

In Britain, the elements of such an organization exist already. The Labour Party and the trade unions would not be alive for twenty days without the continual and largely unrewarded labour of local officials and committeemen—men and woman who without either enormous self-righteousness or heresy-hunting keep the machinery running and save these vast organizations from decay by the divine obstinacy that does not despise addressing envelopes and arguing on doorsteps. Very often they are discontented with their national leaders' timidity, are greeted with mean suspicions at their branch meetings, and find that for candidate they have landed a rich young carpet-bagger from London. They are in fact the storm troops of Labour, but they do not exercise the power and influence which storm troopers deserve, because they are isolated units. Were they in communication and alliance with one another their power would be immense. Nor would it be difficult for any intelligent person at this moment to write down on half a sheet of paper objects on which they would joyfully unite. These objects could (and should) be within the framework of the Labour Party and Trades Union Congress programmes, and might quite well be similar to those mentioned above. But they would be of a definitely revolutionary character—I mean by " revolutionary " that any firm attempt to carry them through would involve a drastic remodelling of society.

To assemble such an organization we must make an appeal of a new kind and secure a new kind of membership. The old type of political organization sought its members anxiously on the high roads. Its cry was " Please join me. You will be asked to do nothing. The subscription is only 1d. a week. All you need do is express sympathy, vote the right way, and read our paper. And if you don't do the last— or even the last two—we won't be unpleasant about it." Such a clarion call assembled practically all the existing Labour or Socialist parties. Our invitation must be the invitation of serious workers to serious workers. It should rather be on the lines of: " If we are satisfied that you are serious, we may allow you to join us." We should admit (to this society whose form is still undecided) only those who are prepared to pledge themselves to work under direction and give a promised amount of time. Whether that time be one evening a week or seven evenings a week is obviously a matter for discussion; but there should be a pledge, and a pledge which is enforced, if we are to exclude the idle and well-intentioned. It would be a disaster for such a body to fail to hold its doors perennially open for all who were willing to accept its objects, for that would be a straight way of becoming a closed corporation of grafters or bureaucrats. But a provision for a pledge would rapidly tire out those who had no real driving enthusiasm behind them and would keep the organization small and wieldy.

Members should suggest themselves what work they can do, for which their private occupations fit them. If they are not able to suggest any, they should put themselves at the orders of the Society, for whatever work it may need done. If they can do neither, though they may vote straight and pay their union dues, they are for our present purposes useless, and we must reject them like Gideon. Nor is it by any means difficult to assign work to them once they are enrolled. Many will be doing it already, as local party executive members, literature sellers, organizers and speakers. There is scarcely anyone, even of the despised middle class, who could not be used or use his peculiar talents. As lawyers advising the unemployed and the local parties, doctors using their knowledge for a labour clinic, film amateurs making revolutionary films and showing them, brainworkers of any kind engaging competently upon the immense problems of research which are at present hopelessly neglected and publishing their results by print or circular, pamphlet writers, social workers

N

collecting cases of injustice and feeding councillors and Members of Parliament with them, clerks running voluntarily in their spare time organizations that need secretarial work—the trouble is not to find work, nor to find workers, but to organize.

It does not seem that without the creation of such an organization of storm troopers or ironsides, which will under no provocation permit itself (as the Communists and I.L.P.'ers have in England) to be isolated from the mass of the workers, that there is any reasonable hope of a social revolution in Great Britain or the United States. There may be yet another disillusioning attempt at " constitutional change " by an unreformed Labour Party in England, or there may not even be that. It seems in the highest degree probable that this will be followed by a general reversion to barbarism and an adaptation of Nazi methods to every country.

Arguments that suggest the possibility[1] of such an organization arrive like the oysters in *Alice* the moment the idea is first entertained. Let us consider the recent history of Germany, the country in which the largest body of " advanced persons " met the most horrible disaster. Why did the German Social-Democratic Party slip slowly down to ruin ? It had been losing its strength, to Communists and Nazis on each side, for months before Hitler's *coup*.

[1] Proposals such as these were put up by the author and others to the British Socialist League in 1933, and after an internal conflict rejected. The author considers this fact of minor importance, but thinks it his duty to mention it.

It was not only that it was itself inert, which was bad enough; it was because it demanded inertia of its members. They had little enough to do but pay their subscriptions, listen to exhortations to support President Hindenburg, and refrain from actions which might embarrass their leaders. But the Nazis and Communists, the moment they enrolled a man, required him to be up and doing. They gave him work to do. Though it might be silly or dangerous work—breaking up trade union meetings or beating Jews, it was still work, and bound him closely to his organization.

The younger generation in particular responds to such an appeal. There is not to-day, though we may regret it, a real enthusiasm for personal liberty. Nobody who has had any considerable acquaintance with the present generation will have failed to notice how slowly it responds to phrases which dwell upon the importance of the individual's personality. The " need for a change of heart," the existence of " a new spirit," the importance of " standing for " this or that principle—these are hollow phrases which by now are almost typical of the more vain and foolish elderly appeal. Men to-day are more anxious to be intelligently ordered and directed than to assert their own individuality; they feel rightly enough that disaster is near, and teamwork is needed to avert it rather than an achievement of individual rectitude. It is a disease typical of those of us who came to maturity during or immediately after the war, to feel as an overwhelming need the necessity to

inspect our own souls, our psychoneuroses, our conscientious objections and our sexual maladjustments.
The later generation is more extroverted and less
introverted: it wishes to do and to be told to do,
not to contemplate.

We must also remember the remarkable successes
achieved by what was on the whole a failure. The
policy of " bolshevisation " within the Communist
International did an enormous amount of damage,
but its insistence on an obligation to work concentrated an equally enormous amount of power
within the Communist Parties. From the years 1923
to 1926, for example, the British Labour movement
was continually shaken by the activities of the British
Communist Party. To read the reports of Labour
Party Conferences and Trades Union Congresses in
those years, and the resolutions that they considered,
you would think that they were resisting the impact
of a party of at least 150,000 members. Now, during
these years, the Communist membership in actual
fact varied between 3,500 and 5,000.

It failed, after causing the most unexampled
upheavals. But it failed not because of its discipline,
but because of three ascertainable gross errors, which
in the future can and should be avoided. The first of
these was that it had, as we have seen, absurd and
self-contradictory " slogans " with which to operate,
decided on by well-intentioned but monstrously
ignorant gentlemen meeting in a medieval fortress
some thousand or two miles away. The second was
that it adopted a policy of secret organization against

its fellow workers, by nucleus work and such devices. Obviously, this can and should be avoided. A truly revolutionary organization may desire to plot against capitalist authority: it cannot plot against its fellow workers. No man should ever deny membership of this suggested League nor should its policies remain hidden and be put up squeakily as in a Punch and Judy show, by puppets whose strings it pulls. Its policies should be avowed and be openly presented and discussed: if they are defeated their advocates should do what they would wish their opponents to do—regret and submit. The third grave error (I am speaking of tactical errors only—fantastically wrong programmes are another matter) was that the Communist Party had parliamentary and municipal ambitions which were bound before long to bring it into conflict with the existing " mass organizations of the workers." There were Labour candidates everywhere: Communist candidates, once put up, became enemy candidates. No League such as this should ever run candidates for any local or national body; it should keep its hands strictly off the proper business of political parties. Were the British Communists in earnest, they would at once adopt this tactic. They would dissolve as a party and re-form as a league or club, sending their members to take out individual cards in the Labour Party and exercise their influence so. They would learn a very great deal about the working class in so doing. If the Third International were really to do what it has sometimes threatened to do—cut off all financial aid,

force the British party to stand on its own legs and
its Central Committee to be directly responsible to its
own rank and file—such development would not be
impossible. Journals which at present exasperate the
division in the workers would quickly collapse, and
the yes-men in office would shortly seek another
easier berth. Unfortunately, so sensible an action by
Moscow is highly unlikely.

It is a condition of all serious revolutionary work
that it shall be carried on by a co-ordinated team.
Nobody, not even a Lenin, can know and control at
once all sides of revolutionary activity. Every serious
advocate of social change must feel himself surrounded by colleagues in whose trusted hands are the
departments that he need not watch. He cannot
be at once an expert on foreign affairs, a writer of
new school text-books and a frustrator of reformist
intrigues inside the local co-op. He must be himself
as serious as the Bolsheviks were in 1917, but he must
also know that others are. He must say: " I, John
Smith, will give up my time and energy, possibly
even my money and my liberty, to the revolution ";
but he is only human and will add: " I will only do
this if I am assured that others around me will do
the same."

To go into greater detail about such an organization would be unnecessary at this time. If the idea is
approved, those who are to form the organization
must take the idea and remould it in accordance with
their needs and knowledge. The author will not even
permit himself to say with certainty that such an

organization will lead to a successful revolution. He can only say, with some confidence, that without it a peaceful (or other) revolution is highly improbable. Further, it seems proved that if no action like this is taken, action of another kind will be taken for us. The working class and the middle class are not to-day likely to suffer and struggle for a spineless Socialist or Labour Party, to put up uncomplainingly with another MacDonald government. The continuance of uncertainty and feebleness will mean that existing organizations will crumble and the disillusioned will drift steadily across to a Fascist organization. Fascism means war; even if it does not, the character of a Fascist State is fairly well known. Once it is established, those who read, who write, who publish or who print, books like this are likely to be dead or in concentration camps.

Would you, who read this, like to be flogged unconscious with a rubber baton ? Perhaps this is an improper question with which to close a serious study. However, it is worthy of thought.

# HOW TO MAKE A REVOLUTION.

By Raymond W. Postgate . . .
*202 pp. . . . New York: The Vanguard Press . . . $1.90.*

Reviewed by
ERNEST SUTHERLAND BATES

MR RAYMOND POSTGATE is an Englishman of distinguished family, a graduate of Oxford, one of the editors of the Encyclopaedia Britannica, formerly a Communist, latterly a member of the British Labor party, author of numerous works ranging from a translation of the *Pervigilium Veneris* to volumes on John Wilkes, Robert Emmett, Karl Marx, Bolshevism and strikes. He writes with ease, humor, clarity and force. A work from his pen on methods of social revolution was certain beforehand to be worth reading. It turns out, in fact, to be peculiarly timely and challenging.

In harmony with his title, "How to Make a Revolution," Mr. Postgate is solely concerned with the relative efficiency of various ways of bringing about a "drastic social change" (his definition of his central term), not at all with the desirability of such a change. Pleasantly aware of the impossibility of scientific certainty in this field, he argues that some at least probable conclusions ought to emerge from an empirical study of actual revolutionary experience. Even here, however, the available evidence is much less than is popularly supposed. Though revolutions have been occurring since the dawn of history, none of them prior to the twentieth century has any relevance to the purposes of this study. The coming of machine guns, tanks, gas and aeroplanes has made the barricades and street-fighting that were still possible fifty years ago today as obsolete as the long bow or the tomahawk.

With his field thus limited for him by the facts, the author takes up the methods advocated by the main forms of modern revolutionary theory—Marxist, syndicalist, anarchist and Blanquist, all four of them proletarian in character. The first, of course, has its double program of parliamentary reform to be supplemented at the appropriate time by military action. The history of parliamentarism, Mr. Postgate finds, indicates that Socialist governments may be fairly successful as long as their reforms keep within the capitalist scheme (in other words, as long as they are not really Socialist), but that sooner or later these governments are overwhelmed by an armed resistance which their previous pacifist career has unfitted them to meet. Syndicalism, recognizing this difficulty, scorning votes and parliaments, puts all its faith in boycotts, sabotage and strikes, but again sooner or later as soon as its strikes even distantly threaten the existence of the capitalist system, syndicalism is forcibly repressed. There remain the methods of anarchism and Blanquism—assassination of government officials by private individuals and the organization of semi-conspiratorial groups to seize the government by a coup d'etat: the former has been repeatedly shown to be futile since no acts of terrorization have ever prevented plenty of other aspirants for office arising to fill the vacant places; the latter has more possibilities but involves a separation from the masses which restricts the Blanquist group to a kind of guerrilla warfare and insures its eventual defeat.

We seem to be left with no other method than that of mass insurrection, but Mr. Postgate proceeds to show that every major government is now in possession of the technological resources to put down almost any conceivable mass insurrection. The general strike, formerly regarded as a revolutionary weapon, has shown itself again and again to be useful for the attainment of limited objectives (among which Mr. Postgate puts the highly important one of preventing war) but once more if it is a really general strike against all industries it brings immediate hardship on the rest of the community and rallies it to support the government in military suppression. Thus peaceful and violent methods alike come to the same impasse where the appeal must be to force while the preponderance of force is hopelessly on the other side.

It would seem almost as if Mr. Postgate's

title should have been, not "How to Make a Revolution" but rather "How Revolutions Can't be Made." Yet in a surprising final chapter, he turns back to the previously rejected method of parliamentary action to argue that with a sufficiently *determined* Socialist party which did not lose sight of its objectives some kind of a revolution might actually be brought about. He does not, apparently, regard such a result as very probable, however, seeming to anticipate instead a universal rule of fascism. Once this is established, he remarks pertinently, "those who read, who write, who publish or who print, books like this are likely to be dead or in concentration camps."

Lest we should cherish any desperate hope that fascism by leading inevitably to war will lead through war to revolution, Mr. Postgate insists that there is no instance in history of a successful war having been followed by revolution and only a very few examples of unsuccessful ones having this result. The normal outcome is simply reaction and a prolonged rule of force. If men are fools enough to go to war in the first place, what likelihood is there that they will become sensible afterwards? Finally, if one maintains that people cannot be held indefinitely in subjection by force, Mr. Postgate brutally replies, "Why not?" "The powers of central authority," he writes, "are more colossal than ever they were before, and yet previous centuries are full of records of people submitting to the rule of force for vast periods of time."

Carefully objective as Mr. Postgate is, and undeniable as are most of his facts, the necessity of his all but completely pessimistic conclusions rests upon certain presuppositions to which he gives scant attention. He assumes that the only possible alternative to a strictly proletarian revolution is a fascist one, and he states, rather than proves, that the lower middle class, which holds the balance of power nearly everywhere today, is irretrievably fascist in disposition. These assumptions are popular; they may be correct; but they need demonstration. That, however, would be a different story, a different book and a different review.